A large furry creature (trainee devoterus), streaked with dirt and grime, bursts into your office. She places a carved wooden object resembling a miniature totem pole in the middle of your polished timber desk. She drags you out of your chair for a bone-crushing bear hug, and declares with wild eyes and panting breath: 'We just got back. I love this kind of training!'

Solemnly, almost ritualistically, she presents you with Thor, the wooden totem of her team, Charlie's Angels. Thor was lovingly carved with the edge of a dull rock by the light of a campfire while the team chanted their new corporate mantra. You muster a mumbled thanks. She hugs you again and tramps off, leaving a trail of dead grass and dirt on the floor. As corporate training manager, you dutifully add Thor to the other icons displayed on your shelves, wisely choosing to give it the most prominent position. After all, this one is from your CEO.

A moment later, another bedraggled soul slumps in peevishly. Ah, you think, trainee negativus. He says what you expect: 'I hated it. You call this training? I didn't learn a thing— except maybe not to climb a pole with tight underwear, and to take more bug repellent if I ever have to do this again'. 'Too bad', you think. This guy is the vice president of human resources—your boss.

Games Trainers Play Outdoors

GARY KROEHNERT

The McGraw-Hill Companies, Inc.

Sydney New York San Francisco Auckland
Bangkok Bogotá Caracas Hong Kong
Kuala Lumpur Lisbon London Madrid
Mexico City Milan New Delhi San Juan
Seoul Singapore Taipei Toronto

McGraw·Hill Australia

A Division of The **McGraw·Hill** Companies

Text © 2002 Gary Kroehnert
Illustrations and design © 2002 McGraw-Hill Australia Pty Ltd
Additional owners of copyright are acknowledged in on-page credits.

Copying for educational purposes

National Library of Australia Cataloguing-in-Publication data:

Kroehnert, Gary.
Games trainers play outdoors.

ISBN 0 074 71211 X.

1. Management games - Study and teaching. 2. Management games - Study and teaching - Australia. 3. Employees - Training of. 4. Active learning. I. Title.

658.312404

Published in Australia by
McGraw-Hill Australia Pty Ltd
4 Barcoo Street, Roseville NSW 2069, Australia
Acquisitions Editor: Javier Dopico
Production Editor: Sybil Kesteven
Editor: Gail Warman
Proofreader: Tim Learner
Design (interior and cover): Greg Gaul
Cartoons and illustrations: Greg Gaul
Typeset in Humanist 521 by Greg Gaul
Printed on 80 gsm woodfree by Pantech Limited, Hong Kong

Contents

RH Risk High	EH Energy High	OU Outdoor	PY Props Yes
RM Risk Medium	EM Energy Medium	IU Indoor	PN Props No
RL Risk Low	EL Energy Low		

Contents

RH Risk High	EH Energy High	OU Outdoor	PY Props Yes
RM Risk Medium	EM Energy Medium	IU Indoor	PN Props No
RL Risk Low	EL Energy Low		

RH Risk High	EH Energy High	OU Outdoor	PY Props Yes
RM Risk Medium	EM Energy Medium	IU Indoor	PN Props No
RL Risk Low	EL Energy Low		

Contents

RH Risk High	EH Energy High	OU Outdoor	PY Props Yes
RM Risk Medium	EM Energy Medium	IU Indoor	PN Props No
RL Risk Low	EL Energy Low		

Introduction

Welcome to the first volume of *Games Trainers Play Outdoors*. After the success of our first set of games books—*100 Training Games*, *101 More Training Games*, *102 Extra Training Games* and *103 Additional Training Games*—it appeared there was a need for a source of games that trainers and facilitators could use outdoors. So here it is!

This book contains seventy-five games, challenges and activities for facilitators to use. There are classic challenges, as well as lots of new activities. Each one has been tried and tested.

Typically when trainers, or trainees, think of outdoor training, they tend to think of the higher-risk activities where people can fall off ropes, trees or logs many metres above the ground—or fall down a cliff face because someone forgot to hold on to something. These are certainly extreme situations. Once this thought is in their mind, they don't want to know anything else about it. However, the level of activity in this book won't have people passing out at the thought of the things they might be asked to do.

We are not saying that some forms of outdoor training aren't high risk, but facilitators need a high degree of training to conduct these activities (and suitable insurance policies to cover any unforeseen circumstance).

The outdoor activities included in this book are focused at low to medium risk. They all create a challenge for the individual or the team. The difference between low, medium and high risk is explained later in this introduction.

There is an assumed link between outdoor training and team building. This assumption is correct in most cases. There is also the added benefit of improving an individual's self-confidence and self-esteem. The long-term benefit of these activities includes higher team productivity, lower turnover rates and a more enjoyable work environment. Teamwork doesn' t just happen because the boss says that they want everyone to work as a team. A team has to learn how to work together.

Here is a classical Chinese story that demonstrates the power of teamwork.

> Once upon a time there was an old man who had ten sons. When he was dying, he called his ten sons over and took out ten chopsticks. He gave each son a chopstick and asked him to try and break it. Each son broke his chopstick without any difficulty. Then the old man took out another ten chopsticks. This time he bundled them up together tightly

and asked each son to try again to break them. None of them could break the ten chopsticks tied together, no matter how hard they each tried. They looked at each other in blank dismay. Then the old man said: 'See, each of you is just like one chopstick. One chopstick is easy to break. If you unite and cooperate, your strength is so great that no one can easily break you'.

There is also a short-term benefit in that participants have a chance to reflect, both as individuals and as a team. In reflecting, they think and talk about what they did during an exercise, what they said, how they said it and how they might do it differently next time.

The main outcomes of any outdoor activities are to:

■ increase the individual's sense of personal confidence

■ increase the team's sense of confidence

■ increase mutual trust within a group

■ improve teamwork

■ improve communication

■ improve interpersonal skills

■ develop increased agility and physical coordination

■ develop increased satisfaction of being with other people

A problem-oriented approach to learning can be useful in developing each individual's awareness of decision-making, leadership, and the strengths and weaknesses of each member within a group.

Disclaimer

Before becoming involved in any form of outdoor training, you need to make certain that you have the knowledge and skill to conduct these activities, and to supply both physical safety and emotional safety for everyone under your control.

We offer the games in this book for your use. However we cannot, and will not, accept any responsibility for the process or outcome of these games. We can observe ten thousand people doing the same activity, with the outcome always being the same. Then one person can do something totally different and unpredictable. These unforeseen events are where some of the risk factors come into play.

Any time you form teams and have an odd number of people left over, use them as spotters or observers. They can help you with safety issues and can make additional observations you may have missed.

Although the activities in this book are shown in a step-by-step format, regard what is printed in these steps as suggestions only. We encourage you to modify them. Use your imagination and be creative with them!

Facilitators' responsibilities

Facilitators of the activities in this book must take total responsibility for their selection and use. The facilitator selects the location, and is the one watching people on the day. Facilitators must be observant at all times: they must watch everything and everyone without exception. If something is going wrong, they are responsible for taking control and looking after participants' safety and wellbeing. The facilitator is responsible for minimising participants' emotional upset or physical harm.

As a facilitator, you are also responsible for telling participants what to wear to your programs. Have them wear appropriate clothing and footwear. Jeans, shorts, tee-shirts, singlets, sweatshirts and sneakers are all suitable for most of the outdoor activities shown here. Don't forget to also suggest a baseball cap or hat, and some sunblock (although make sure you have some in your first aid kit for anyone who needs it and has forgotten to bring any).

As we have just suggested, you should also have a well-stocked first aid kit. It's like going on a picnic with a group of children—someone will scrape their knee or cut their finger, so be prepared.

Make sure you have a stopwatch and a whistle. These are standard items of equipment for outdoor training.

In several activities, we suggest that blindfolded participants assume the 'bumper' position. This is where they bend their elbows and hold their hands and arms up, palms facing outward at about face height. This will protect their upper body if they accidentally bump into anything. Have participants assume the 'bumper' position whenever this is a possibility.

The game Preventing Injury shows participants how to fall correctly. This game is included both as an outdoor activity and for safety reasons: it's there for fun, and to show people how to protect themselves should they accidentally fall during any of the challenges (the terms challenge, activity, initiative and exercise are all synonymous in this book).

We also suggest facilitators use spotters in some activities. Falls are to be expected. Proper spotting will prevent a fall from causing injury. A spotter's main role is to closely watch other participants in any activity, so the spotter can give them some protection should they happen to fall. The spotter's first priority is to protect the participant's head and upper body by offering physical support. If you think you need spotters for any exercise, use them! But try to avoid using so many that they outnumber the participants, or get in each other's way, or prevent people from falling off balance in a squatting position (see the game Preventing Injury as an example). Help can be taken too far in some cases!

It's imperative that facilitators address any safety and sensitivity issues when they brief participants, and they should be aware that not all games will suit all groups. Safety issues must be stated at the outset of any program and reinforced during the program.

Having said all of that, outdoor training is a huge amount of fun for everyone if it's conducted in a safe manner. It will certainly keep you on your toes and,

although you probably won't be participating in many of the activities yourself, you will more than likely feel more exhausted than the participants at the end of the day!

By now, we imagine that those of you with less experience as facilitators are feeling a range of emotions. Perhaps you're feeling nervous, scared, apprehensive, excited or anxious. These feelings are not unusual. Whether you have led a team exercise before or not, the main thing is to relax! Take a deep breath and enjoy the experience.

We should also mention that any person who doesn't want to participate in any activity should be allowed to withdraw. No one should be forced to participate in anything they don't feel comfortable attempting. If this happens, they can be used as observers—the extra pair of eyes can come in handy. However, generally we find that people who choose not to participate initially want to try something with team members later. Usually, their team members will encourage them, and you find that they're swinging on the ropes in no time!

'Scripted' briefings are included with some activities. These are suggestions only. Please modify them or create your own. They have been included to get you thinking creatively. Any briefings given should create, or add to, a fantasy. For example, the briefing for the first game, Spider's Web, should have participants imagining a spider hiding in the tree waiting for them: they should almost be able to see it, so set the scene for them by painting a verbal picture and using appropriate props where they are available. Use your imagination!

Outdoor training: What is it?

What is outdoor training or outdoor learning? What makes it a valuable learning experience? Does it work? And, if it does work, how does it work and for whom?

Outdoor learning is any learning activity, exercise or simulation that can be conducted outside the classroom environment—that is, out of the traditional learning environment.

There are two distinct types of outdoor learning. One is generally referred to as 'adventure training', and includes high-risk activities or perceived high-risk activities. The other uses low-risk activities and is generally referred to as 'outdoor learning' or 'outdoor training'.

Outdoor learning conjures up many different pictures to many different people.

Outdoor training can be seen as an ongoing professional development program for seasoned executives or used as a resource to meet the special challenges of transition management during reorganisation. More often, it is used to improve cooperation, develop trust, improve teams and build confidence in training groups, work groups or individuals. Challenges or activities are designed according to desired program outcomes.

Outdoor training promotes many team-centred activities and individual development activities. These activities include ropes activities, skirmish, paintball, hang-gliding, bushwalking, camping, scuba diving, windsurfing, motor sports, skydiving, grass skiing, sailboarding, rollerblading, canoeing, bush trail rides, and simulations. There are many others.

It is worth reflecting on the origins of the word 'team'. The dominant image for us today is the sports team in football, baseball, hockey or cricket. But originally, for the Anglo-Saxons, a team meant a family or offspring. It was applied to several draught animals harnessed in a row because oxen pull better together when they are related. From those teams of oxen came the use of team to describe a number of persons in concerted action:

Together

Everybody

Achieves

More

Features of outdoor training

Does outdoor training make any difference in participants' attitudes and work behaviours? Does it affect organisational outcomes? The whole issue is open to question. Many trainers believe this type of training does work, provided the rules for all types of effective training programs are respected. These include clear objectives, skilled facilitation, a plan to transfer the knowledge gained back to the job, and credible evaluation and follow-up.

Most outdoor training programs are conducted for team initiative and group problem-solving exercises. Current research indicates that the focus of wilderness programs is primarily on leadership and decision-making (60% and 40% respectively). In contrast, the objectives of outdoor-centred programs are much more wide ranging. They include team building (90%), self-esteem (50%), leadership (40%), problem-solving (20%), decision-making (15%) and encouraging a sense of corporate ownership (2%).

High-risk and low-risk activities

Outdoor learning combines cognitive learning with subjective interpretations based on the individual's feelings, attitudes and values. The vast majority of experiential exercises used in outdoor learning programs are high-risk activities. A generally accepted definition of a high-risk activity is one where participants may be higher than eye level above the ground and perceive a risk of danger or injury to themselves. A low-risk activity is one where participants are no higher than eye level above the ground and perceive the activity to be almost accident-free. A third category, medium-risk activity, is where participants are no higher than eye-level from the ground but perceive risk to themselves or their team.

Most high-risk activities were originally designed to develop the individual, whereas lower-risk activities highlight the need for improved teamwork, and problem-solving, decision-making and communication skills. This is still generally true.

Examples of high-risk activities include orienteering, cross-country navigation, abseiling, whitewater rafting, cross-country skiing, zip wires and high ropes courses. Examples of low-risk activities include simulations such as Spider Web, Kangaroo Races, Minefield and The Moat (all in this book), and trust walks. Many other low-risk activities are shown in our other training games books, *100 Training Games*, *101 More Training Games*, *102 Extra Training Games* and *103 Additional Training Games*. Although the games in these books are generally designed for indoor use, many of them can be adapted for use outdoors to supplement your training activities. For example, you can use them as part of the debriefing process or to extend a program when extra time is available. They can also come in handy if the weather is so bad that you can't get anyone to go outside!

Throughout this book you will see symbols at the top of the first page of each game. They indicate the level of risk and energy required; whether the games are for use outdoors or indoors; and whether props are required to play the game.

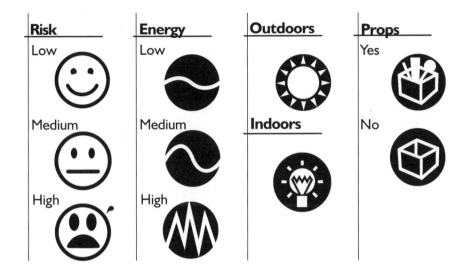

Risk	Energy	Outdoors	Props
Low	Low		Yes
Medium	Medium	Indoors	No
High	High		

What makes a good program?

Briefing and debriefing

Most successful outdoor learning programs usually begin with detailed introductions or orientations, although some have very little in the way of information at the start. They all have thorough debriefings that link back to the workplace or other appropriate place.

In any team briefing, there are three requests facilitators should make of the group and have the group agree to. They are:

1. To work together as a team towards team and individual goals.
2. To look after the safety and wellbeing of themselves and fellow team members.
3. To give and receive feedback to improve the future performance of both themselves and their team members.

Although we suggest a few debriefing questions with each activity, additional questions might cover issues such as:

■ Leadership: how much and what styles

■ Delegation: how it's best done

■ Teamwork: the benefits and how to improve it

■ Trust: how to develop it

■ Team support: why it's necessary and how to create it

■ Conflict: what to do about it and how to resolve it

■ Peer pressure: its impact

■ Communication: what the problems are and how to improve it

■ Competition: identifying who the competition is and clarifying assumptions

■ Sexism: the roles people perceive or play

■ Stereotypes: the effect they have

■ Fears: what they are

■ Joy: what creates it

■ Self-confidence: its benefits and how to improve it

■ Follow-through: how to use it back in the workplace

Clear objectives

Outdoor training programs, like all other programs, need to have clearly defined objectives before training commences. Both trainers and organisations must be conscious of the fact that these programs may have only entertainment value if they are not properly designed. Poor design may result in participants not learning anything but saying they had a good time. If your only aim for the program was for participants to have a good time, then it could be seen as a success!

Is there a sequence?

The first attempt at a formal outdoor-based training program took place in 1941. Outdoor programs first began to attract corporate attention around the world in the late 1970s and early 1980s. They have grown dramatically in popularity since then. Originally, formal outdoor-based learning was centred on the development of individual skills rather than having a team-centred approach. This now seems to have altered.

We still see the focus on the individual when outdoor-based learning is used to develop higher-level leadership skills. Although some leadership skills can be developed in a team situation, the higher one gets in most organisations, the more individual attention may be required to find or improve these leadership skills.

The four levels of application for outdoor training are set out below.

First level   Traditional classroom-based training activities

Imparts general knowledge and skills required to perform specific duties and tasks.

Second level   Lower-risk outdoor training activities, incorporating group problem-solving challenges

Targets the development of improved organisational communication. Used to improve cooperation, improve teamwork and build confidence in specific training groups. Example activity: Spider's Web

Third level   Lower-risk outdoor training activities, incorporating individual challenges requiring team support

Similar to the second level but far more emphasis on activities requiring team support and developing trust. Example activity: All Tied Up

Fourth level   Higher-risk outdoor training activities and wilderness programs

Takes on the role of allowing individual participants to discover more about themselves and their relationships with others, to gain new insights into their abilities and potential, to develop self-reliance, resourcefulness and determination to succeed, and to enhance self-motivation and raise personal standards of achievement. Example activity: Trust Fall

The table shows the first level of training as being traditional classroom based training applications. This level imparts general knowledge and skills required to perform specific duties and tasks. The second level shows the application of lower-risk outdoor-based training. This level targets the development of improved organisational communication. It is used to improve cooperation, improve teamwork and build confidence in training groups. The third level develops trust within teams. It also develops team support. The fourth level takes on the role of allowing participants to discover more about themselves and their relationships with others, to gain new insights into their abilities and potential, to develop self-reliance, resourcefulness and determination to succeed, and to enhance self-motivation and raise personal standards of achievement.

Defining levels in this way is not an attempt to suggest that any one level is better than another. What it does attempt to do is show the progression of outdoor training applications. It would also appear that some organisations and some countries may be operating at different levels, both for the right and wrong reasons.

There would appear to be three ways people change on these programs. They are through shock, through evolution or through anticipation. Each has its own application. This needs to be considered along with the different levels shown above.

> *If you put a frog in a pan of hot water he jumps right out, but if you put him in a pan of cold water he just swims around even though you turn the heat up a little by little. He adapts ... right to frog legs.*

Designing your program

To design a highly relevant outdoor training program, facilitators must find out exactly what the work group or individual sees as their strengths and weaknesses, and what kinds of problems need to be addressed. The games used in these programs need to been seen as challenges for the individual or the team, or perhaps both.

Facilitators must also ascertain the level of outdoor learning activities that is best suited to each situation. The outcomes must also be limited to a reasonable number, say one or two, not a fix-all for everything.

When designing the sequence of a program it's good to use activities that help set the stage for what's to come next. As a general rule of thumb, start with an icebreaking activity which allows people to get to know one another. Follow this with a disinhibiting activity, which encourages the group to do something a bit out of the ordinary. The third step would be spotting and trust activities. This sequence culminates in the initiatives themselves.

When dealing with larger groups, think about the possibility of using a challenge circuit. Start the program off with everyone participating in the icebreakers and disinhibiters, but then have people separate into teams and go through a circuit of challenges. You could have several of these set up in different locations using different facilitators. The facilitators would debrief each activity with each group. These activities could include, for example, Spider's Web, Nitro Crossing, Escape from Alcatraz, Siamese Soccer, The Moat and Cosmic Slop. If you plan the activities well, you could even have teams exchange members in between challenges. After everyone has completed the circuit, bring them back together for a group debriefing session.

It's important to stress the application of the training program to participants' present and future workplace or work team. On the surface, some of these activities may seem to have a high level of entertainment value. They do. We make no apology for that. But it is essential that the trainer facilitate before, during and particularly after any activity to ensure that participants see the activity's relevance. For this reason it's a good idea for facilitators to test any activity before using it with a 'real' group. You must ensure that you are familiar with any activity before attempting to use it.

As a facilitator, you will be working with a group of people unique in their demands and requests. Not every participant in an exercise will demand the same treatment or explanation but, as a facilitator, you must expect the unexpected.

It may not always be appropriate to let participants select their own teams or partners. They will have preferences as to whom they want to be with. Encourage them to mix, but do it subtly. You may even design activities so that sworn enemies finish up having to work together in a cooperative exercise.

Outdoor training is still a relatively new field. It has plenty of room to grow and to demonstrate its strengths if future programs are designed and implemented correctly.

Use the following games wisely, and keep your BODS in mind:

Brief the activity

Observe the group

Debrief the activity

Safety issues

Good training and good luck!

Gary Kroehnert
May 2002
Dr Gary Kroehnert
PO Box 3169
Grose Vale NSW 2753
Australia
Phone: (02) 4576 0800
Fax: (02) 4576 0700
Email: doctorgary@hotmail.com

Games Codes Grid

Game	Page	Risk High	Risk Medium	Risk Low	Energy High	Energy Medium	Energy Low	Outdoor Use	Indoor Use	Props Yes	Props No
1. Spider's Web	1		•			•		•		•	
2. Nitro Crossing	5		•		•			•		•	
3. Score Three	8			•		•		•		•	
4. POW	11			•			•	•	•	•	
5. Single Knots	15			•			•	•		•	
6. Raiders of the Lost Ark	17		•		•			•		•	
7. Outdoor Game Design	20			•		•		•		•	
8. Balloon Races	22			•	•			•		•	
9. New Talent	24			•				•	•		•
10. Minefield	26	•				•		•	•		•
11. Ladders 'R' Us	29	•				•		•	•	•	
12. Name Game	31			•		•		•		•	
13. Tied in Knots	33			•		•		•			•
14. Moving Balls	36			•		•		•		•	
15. Bouncing Beach Ball	39			•	•			•		•	
16. Pulse Speed	41			•		•		•	•		•
17. Trapped	43	•				•		•		•	
18. Marshmallowed	46		•		•			•		•	
19. Polo Balloon	49			•	•			•		•	
20. Step Right In	52			•		•		•	•		•
21. Dynamite	54		•			•		•	•	•	

Games Codes Grid

Game	Page	Risk High	Risk Medium	Risk Low	Energy High	Energy Medium	Energy Low	Outdoor Use	Indoor Use	Props Yes	Props No
22. Recycle Ball	57			•		•		•		•	
23. Tents 'R' Us	60	•				•		•		•	
24. Hoops Away	63			•		•		•	•	•	
25. Catch What You Can	65		•			•		•		•	
26. Rollin', Rollin', Rollin'	67	•			•			•	•	•	
27. Sightless Soccer	70	•			•			•		•	
28. Tuber	73		•		•			•		•	
29. Hide and Seek	77		•			•		•		•	
30. Human Machines	80			•		•		•			•
31. Pass the Life Saver®	82			•			•	•	•	•	
32. Bricks Galore	84			•		•		•		•	
33. Stepping In	87		•			•		•		•	
34. Abstract Web	90			•		•		•	•	•	
35. Kangaroo Races	92			•		•		•		•	
36. Trust Fall	94	•				•		•		•	
37. Preventing Injury	98		•			•		•			•
38. Marooned	101			•		•			•	•	•
39. Sound Walk	104	•				•		•		•	
40. Stretching the Imagination	107			•		•		•	•	•	
41. Bumper Wall	110	•				•		•		•	
42. All Tied Up	113		•			•		•		•	

Games Codes Grid

Games Codes Grid

Game	Page	Risk High	Risk Medium	Risk Low	Energy High	Energy Medium	Energy Low	Outdoor Use	Indoor Use	Props Yes	Props No
64. Water Balloon Ball	172		•			•		•		•	
65. Contagious	174			•		•		•		•	
66. Siamese Soccer	176			•	•			•		•	
67. Butt to Butt	178			•		•		•	•		•
68. South Pacific	181			•	•			•		•	
69. Sherlock Holmes	183			•			•		•		•
70. Tidal Wave	185	•				•		•	•		•
71. Greed	188			•	•			•		•	
72. Cosmic Slop	189		•			•		•		•	
73. Phoenix	194	•		•			•		•		
74. Life on a String	197	•				•		•		•	
75. Escape from Alcatraz	201	•				•		•		•	

1. Spider's Web

Time required

1 hour plus.

Size of group

Unlimited, but large groups need to be broken into smaller teams of 8 to 12 participants.

Material required (for each team)

2 trees large enough not to bend easily (to support the web).

Plenty of nylon cord, fishing line or similar (to make the web).

8 large staples, eye bolts, electrical ties or pieces of rope (to hold the web on the tree).

Enough blindfolds for participants who get bitten by the spider.

Optional: small bells to use as warning devices; a large rubber spider (for decoration).

Overview

This famous outdoor activity is probably one of the best known team building exercises around. It has an excellent mix of challenge and fantasy. It can be used for team building, teamwork, conflict resolution, leadership skills and communication skills. It requires a reasonable amount of preparation by the facilitator, but it's more than worth the effort.

Goals

1. To develop teamwork.
2. To improve communication.
3. To demonstrate the benefit of synergy (working together).
4. To bond participants.
5. To solve a seemingly impossible problem.

Spider's Web

Preparation

1. The facilitator needs to set up a Spider Web for each team.

2. Start by making 8 anchor points (very large staples, eye bolts, electrical ties or simply pieces of rope tied around the tree trunk) in 2 trees (4 in each tree). The lowest anchor point should be about 20 cm (8 inches) from ground level. Make 3 more anchor points at 70 cm (2 feet 4 inches) intervals so that the highest is about 2.3 metres (7 feet 8 inches) above the ground (see figure 1).

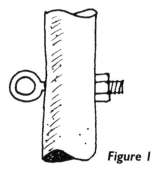

Figure 1

3. Once you have secured the 8 anchor points, measure how much nylon line is required to run up the 4 points on one tree, across to the top anchor point on the other tree, down the anchor points on that tree, then across to the bottom anchor point on the

first tree. It's a good idea to tie knots about 10 to 15 cm (4 to 6 inches) apart along the full length of the line before putting it up. This will give you plenty of points to tie the inner web to so that it doesn't slip (see figure 2).

Knot to stop 'Web' slipping

Figure 2

4. Tie the line to the bottom anchor point of the first tree, then run it up the first tree's anchor points, across to the second tree, down the second tree's anchor points, and across to your starting point. Tie the line off so that it's tight and secure.

5. Now that the outside of the web is in place, you can start to fill it in. It's best to tie off near one corner and work from there. What you're after is something that resembles a spider's web, with just enough openings in

the web that are large enough for people to fit through (see main figure).

6. When the web is complete, you can tie a rubber spider and bells on to it (if you use them). The rubber spider adds to the fantasy, and the bells will serve as a warning device should participants disturb the web during the exercise.

Procedure

1. Break a large group into smaller teams of 8 to 12 participants.

2. Brief the teams about the activity. The briefing will go something like this:

Your team has been trapped in a forest. The only way out of the forest is to go through the Spider Web (that's through it—not around it, over it or under it). Fortunately the spider is sleeping at present, but unfortunately the spider is a very light sleeper. If anyone touches the web, even slightly, while trying to pass through it, the spider will wake up and bite them. The bite of this spider causes immediate blindness to the person bitten and any team member who has already passed through the web. Once a team member has passed through a hole in the web, that hole can no longer be used. This means that every person must use a different hole.

3. If there are several teams, have each team watch the others when they finish their game.

4. When all teams have completed the exercise, you can lead a discussion about issues such as teamwork, communications, conflict and leadership.

Sample debriefing questions

What problems did you encounter?

How did you break down problems? Who did what?

How did you overcome problems?

What helped to achieve the result?

Was there any conflict? How did you deal with it?

Did any leaders emerge? Were others forced to take over? How did they feel about this?

What does this exercise demonstrate?

How does this activity relate to the workplace?

Safety issues

Participants should not be allowed to dive through the Spider's Web openings.

Variations

1. It's more than okay to change the rules as the exercise progresses. Rule changes should increase the challenge of the activity.

2. Rather than participants being 'blinded' if they touch the Spider's Web while passing though it, it could affect their vocal cords so they can't speak anymore.

3. If you see someone taking complete control of the exercise and you want to stop them, have the spider spit at them so they are blinded or lose their voice. This can be permanent (for the duration of the activity) or for a predetermined time, say 5 minutes. This should ensure someone else takes over the leadership role.

4. If this activity is to be used more than once, it may be worthwhile making a frame for the Spider's Web out of PVC pipe. Drill the pipe ready for the web to be tied off. After use, pull it apart and pack it up ready for use the next time.

5. To increase the challenge, you may also require each team to take a full bucket of water with them through the web. This can be introduced as a special antitoxin that can be used (if anyone gets bitten) once the entire team is through the web.

Facilitator's notes

Time required

30 minutes to
1 hour.

Size of group

Unlimited, but
large groups need
to be broken into
smaller teams of 8
to 12 participants.

Material required (for each team)

1 tall tree with
branches (to tie a
swing rope on).

1 length of rope
(the swing rope)
that is strong
enough to take the
weight of the
heaviest
participant.

2 lengths of timber,
4 to 6 metres (12
to 20 feet) long, or
2 lengths of string
and 4 stakes (to
mark the 'river
banks').

1 bucket of water
(the 'nitro').

Spare water to top
up the bucket.

Overview

This activity will get participants
thinking and their blood moving.
It's focused on teamwork, planning
and communication.

Goals

1. To improve teamwork.
2. To involve the team in a
    problem-solving exercise.

Preparation

1. You need to set up a swing
    rope that enables
    participants to swing from
    the tree to an area marked
    out as the 'river banks'. Once
    you have selected a suitable
    tree branch (make sure it is
    strong enough), tie the rope
    securely to it. The rope
    should be long enough to

reach the area beyond the 'river banks'.

2. Work out the preferred direction for participants to swing. At each end of the swing area, place a length of timber or string on the ground to indicate the banks of the river. If string is used, it's best to put 2 stakes out along each 'river bank', tie the string between them and fasten the string so it's taut.

3. Fill up each team's bucket with water to within 2 or 3 cm (about 1 inch) from the top. This will be their bucket of 'nitro'.

Procedure

1. Once the teams have been formed, they need to be briefed on the activity. The briefing could be something like this:

You have been in the outback looking for precious metals and stones. Your group was doing some digging, and the cave you were in partly collapsed. Your team was able to get out, but unfortunately there are still some people trapped. The only hope of getting them out is to blast through the rubble that has fallen.

You were able to get back to your main camp and get this bucket of nitro. You now have to get back to the cave site. The problem is that you now have to cross a river that is infested with crocodiles. There is a rope that can be used to swing across. You need to get the bucket (and its contents) across the river without spilling a drop. You also need to get the whole team over as well. If you happen to spill anything, even a drop, from the bucket, you will have to come back and start over again. If anyone touches the surface of the river they will be eaten by crocodiles. Again, if this happens the team will have to start over again. Your first challenge is to get the rope that is hanging in the middle of the river. Remember, no one is allowed to touch the water.

2. Once the exercise is complete, you can lead a discussion about issues such as teamwork and problem-solving.

Sample debriefing questions

What was the problem? How was it broken down? Who did what?

What helped to achieve the result?

What problems did you encounter? How did you overcome them?

Did any leaders emerge?

What does this exercise demonstrate?

How does this activity relate to the workplace?

Safety issues

Usually knots are not allowed to be tied in the swing rope. If your participants are reluctant or young, it may be worth while putting one knot near the end of the rope about 1 metre (3 feet) above ground level so that they can put the rope between their legs to help support them.

Variations

1. You can set a time limit for the activity, saying that there is only enough air left in the cave for a certain amount of time.

2. This activity can be conducted indoors, using a climbing rope in a gymnasium.

Facilitator's notes

3. Score Three

Estimated time required

5 to 10 minutes.

Size of group

Unlimited.

Material required

1 large garbage bin (to throw balls in)

40 tennis balls in a bag or box (to throw in the garbage bin)

Overview

A quick activity to help participants see the benefit of using clear directions.

Goal

To demonstrate how good communication can improve results.

Procedure

1. Start this exercise by asking for a volunteer. Have the volunteer come to the front of the group with you.

2. Have your volunteer stay looking in one direction. Tell them that they are not allowed to turn around. Give them the bag of tennis balls.

3. Place the garbage bin about 10 metres (30 feet) away from them. Try not to put the bin directly behind them, but slightly off centre in either direction.

4. Tell your volunteer that it's their job to throw the tennis balls over their shoulder and have them land in the bin. Again, tell them that they are not allowed to turn around to see how they are doing. Advise them that they must get at least 3 in the bin to be successful.

5. Let the group know that they can give any verbal directions they feel necessary to help achieve the result.

6. Once the volunteer has thrown 3 balls into the bin (and this may take several attempts), ask what helped them to achieve the goal and what happened to make it more difficult. Ask the group whether they feel a sense of achievement also.

7. Lead a discussion about ways of improving instructions or communication in the workplace.

Sample debriefing questions

What helped to achieve the goal?

What happened to make it more difficult?

Did those who gave instructions, as well as the 'thrower', feel as though they achieved the goal?

How could we get a better or faster result?

What does this exercise demonstrate?

How does this activity relate to the workplace?

Safety issues

Make certain that no one is hit by flying balls.

Variations

It can be useful to blindfold your volunteer, as well as having their back turned away from the garbage bin, as this creates more confusion when team members give directions such as 'to the left' and 'slightly right'.

Facilitator's notes

4. POW

Time required

2 to 3 minutes to introduce and brief the team, plus time to solve the exercise (this can vary dramatically between groups).

Size of group

Unlimited, but large groups need to be broken into teams of 4 participants.

Material required

2 red hats, each one in a heavyweight paper bag (for 2 volunteers to wear).

2 blue hats, each one in a heavyweight paper bag (for another 2 volunteers to wear).

1 solid brick wall or large tree (to separate one volunteer from the other 3).

Overview

Here is an exercise to get everyone in the group thinking. It can be used for teamwork, communication or simply for fun.

Goals

1. To demonstrate the benefit of using a team to solve a problem.

2. To have some fun.

3. To give participants a problem to solve overnight on courses that are run for more than one day.

Preparation

Put each coloured hat in a paper bag (so that the volunteers will not see them) but mark the bags so that you make sure you give the first 'prisoner' a red hat, the second prisoner a blue hat, the third prisoner a red hat and the fourth prisoner a blue hat.

Procedure

1. Introduce this activity by telling the group that they are going to be given a problem to solve.

11

2. Ask for 4 volunteers to be 'prisoners'. Give each volunteer their paper bag, and tell them not to open it until you ask them to.

3. Position the 4 volunteers as shown in the diagram on the previous page. The first 'prisoner' stands behind a solid brick wall (or large tree) and will be wearing a red hat. The second prisoner stands on the other side of the wall, facing the wall. They will be wearing a blue hat. The third prisoner stands behind the second prisoner, facing their back, and will be wearing a red hat. The fourth prisoner stands behind the third, again facing their back, and will be wearing a blue hat. Once they're in position, tell them that they are not allowed to turn around or talk under any circumstance.

4. Have everyone else form teams of 4, and ask them to remain silent and to listen in.

5. Once everyone is in position, brief your 4 volunteers. The briefing will go something like this:

I would like you to imagine that you're being held as prisoners in a POW camp. The camp commandant has asked the 4 of you to stand in a set sequence wearing a hat. You are not allowed to move or turn around. You are not allowed to talk. If you turn around or talk, you will all be shot immediately. Please close your eyes, take your hat out of your bag and put it on your head. No one must look at their own hat. The commandant is now going to give you a challenge. If one of the 4 prisoners can tell him what colour hat he has on his head he will let all of you go. However, if the first answer is not correct you will all be shot. You must remember that you are not allowed to talk, move or turn around. Therefore the first answer given will determine your fate. One vital piece of information to get you started is that there are 2 red hats and 2 blue hats.

6. Read the brief again. Once your volunteers understand what is required, say to them: 'The next word uttered by any one of you will seal your fate. Good luck!'.

7. Now send the other teams out of earshot, and ask them

to work out which prisoner can answer this problem correctly, and why.

8. After one team has solved the problem, you can lead a discussion about teamwork, communication and problem-solving.

Sample debriefing questions

What was the problem? How was it broken down? Who did what?

What does this exercise demonstrate?

How does this activity relate to the workplace?

Variations

1. The story can be modified to suit different groups.
2. Each team of 4 can be set up as described, but this may take a lot of time and would require more hats.
3. This can be a problem-solving activity for teams to work on overnight on courses that are for more than one day.

Solution

Prisoner number 3 is the only one who can solve this problem. They can see that the prisoner in front of them (prisoner number 2) is wearing a blue hat. Prisoner number 3 knows that if both prisoners numbers 2 and 3 were wearing blue hats, prisoner number 4 would see the 2 blue hats and know that their own hat was red. But as prisoner number 4 has said nothing, it means that prisoner number 4 must see both a red hat and a blue hat. Therefore, as prisoner number 3 can see a blue hat in front of them, it means that prisoner number 3's own hat must be red.

Facilitator's notes

If there is any possibility of any of the 4 participants seeing their own hat before they put it on their head, it may be advisable for the facilitator to hold on to all of the hats and place them on their heads for them. This activity will obviously not work if participants see the colour of their hat beforehand.

5. Single Knots

Time required

2 to 10 minutes.

Size of group

Unlimited, but large groups need to be broken into smaller teams of 5 to 7 participants.

Material required (for each team)

A piece of rope about 1 metre (3 feet) long.

Overview

A simple activity that can be used at any time during outdoor training.

Goals

1. To clear participants' minds before a break.
2. To demonstrate the benefit of synergy (working together).
3. To have some fun.

Procedure

1. Tell the group they are going to be given a simple problem to solve.
2. Break a large group into smaller teams of 5 to 7 participants.
3. Hand each team a length of rope.

4. Brief the teams about the activity. The briefing will go something like this:

There is old legend about an ancient magician who learnt how to tie a knot in a piece of rope while holding on to both ends of it—that is, one end of the rope in each hand. The first time she did this, she was so pleased that she stopped for a cup of coffee to reflect on what she had accomplished. Your team's job is to work out how this was done and then have a cup of coffee and reflect on what we've done so far on the course.

5. As each team solves the problem, they can go straight to the break.

Variations

Can be conducted as an individual exercise.

Solution

Have one person fold their arms across their chest. Then give them the free ends of the rope in each hand. As they unfold their arms, the rope will automatically knot itself.

Facilitator's notes

6. Raiders of the Lost Ark

Time required

30 to 60 minutes depending on the size and skill of the group.

Size of group

Unlimited, but large groups need to be broken into teams of 10 to 16 participants.

Material required (for each team)

1 length of rope about 6 metres (20 feet) long.

2 trees about 150 mm (6 inches) in diameter and 4 or 5 metres (12 to 15 feet) apart.

Optional: 1 large rubber spider (for decoration).

Overview

Here is a team initiative that requires everyone to participate.

Goals

1. To have everyone involved in a team challenge.

2. To build trust within the team.

3. To have participants interact physically without being self-conscious.

Preparation

Set up this activity before the program commences. Tie the rope off on one tree about 1.5 metres (5 feet) above ground level. Take the rope to the other tree and tie it off at the same height, keeping the rope taut between the trees. If you use the rubber spider, hang it from the centre of the rope for effect.

If this is to be part of a permanent course, replace the rope with a length of straight tree trunk about 15 cm (6 inches) in diameter and bolt it to the 2 trees.

Procedure

1. Brief the teams. Your briefing could go something like this:

Those of you who saw Raiders of the Lost Ark will remember there was a section in the cave that had lots of trip wires. What happened if someone touched the trip wires? Poison arrows were fired out of concealed openings in the walls. What we have here is a training challenge for people who might be planning to undertake an expedition like that in the future. Imagine that the ropes tied between the 2 trees are trip wires inside a cave. Your entire team needs to cross over the rope without touching it. If anyone touches it, everyone will end up with dozens of poisonous darts sticking out of them. To be successful, you must go over the rope without touching it. Good luck!.

2. If anyone touches the rope during the activity, have the entire team start again.

Sample debriefing questions

How successful were the teams at completing the challenge?

What was the problem? How did you break it down?

What roles did people take?

Did the teams work effectively together? Why?

What problems did you encounter? How did you overcome them?

What helped the teams to perform the task?

Safety issues

Keep an eye on everyone for this challenge (and listen in at the same time). People will try anything to cross over the rope and forget about safety issues if you let them. Taking a running jump to cross over the rope is one obvious solution the group will come up with, however this is not allowed.

Rather than simply disallowing it though, be creative—tell the team that someone must have touched a trip wire and the earth has turned into a sticky clay making it impossible to run.

Variations

If you need to challenge the teams further, blindfold one or 2 team members to make this activity much more difficult.

Facilitator's notes

7. Outdoor Game Design

Time required

45 to 60 minutes.

Size of group

Unlimited, but large groups need to be broken into smaller teams of 5 to 7 participants.

Material required (for each team)

1 large ball, e.g. a soccer ball or basketball

2 small balls, e.g. tennis balls

2 broom handles

3 lengths of rope, each 3 to 6 metres long (10 to 20 feet)

4 sheets of A3 paper

Overview

This activity is designed to get the whole team thinking creatively.

Goals

1. To show the benefits of team members working together.
2. To encourage creativity.
3. To develop a team approach to problem-solving.

Procedure

1. Ask people to form teams of 5 to 7 participants.
2. Give each team the set of materials required.
3. Tell the teams that they have 30 minutes to design a brand new game using the materials provided. At the end of the 30 minutes, each team is to describe their game. Participants will vote to decide which is the best game, and then everyone will play it!
4. The briefing will go something like this:

Our company has been producing and selling outdoor games for many years. The CEO is concerned that nothing new has been developed recently. Unfortunately the last game we developed was a complete failure.

As a result, we have a lot of surplus materials that we haven't been able to sell. The CEO has requested that each team create a brand new game, utilising the resources we have left in stock. The CEO will be here in 30 minutes and expects to hear about a new game from each team. Any team not meeting the CEO's expectations will go straight to gaol and not pass go. Obviously each game should have a name that can be used for marketing purposes. After we decide which game design is best, you will be allowed to test the game to see if you still like it.

Sample debriefing questions

What was the problem? How was it broken down? Who did what?

What problems did you encounter? How did you overcome them?

How does this activity relate to the workplace?

Safety issues

These will be specific to the games designed by the teams.

Variations

All materials may be changed to suit the situation or what's available.

Facilitator's notes

Time required

5 minutes.

Size of group

Unlimited.

Material required

1 balloon for each pair of participants, plus a few spares.

2 lengths of rope (to mark the start and finish lines).

Overview

This is a lively activity to get the blood flowing.

Goals

1. To energise the group.
2. To demonstrate cooperative power.
3. To have some fun.

Procedure

1. Select a suitable place for a relay race, preferably a flat and level area.

2. Start by asking everyone in the group to select a partner.

3. Give each pair a balloon.

4. Ask them to fully inflate the balloon and tie it off.

5. Lay the 2 lengths of rope along the ground about 20 metres (60 feet) apart— the further the better, but they shouldn't be 1000 metres apart! The ropes mark the starting and finishing lines.

6. Ask all participants to stand behind the starting line.

7. Tell them that they will be having a relay race. To win, they have to be the first pair to get to the finishing line and then return to the starting line with their balloon.

8. The rules are: their balloon must be intact when they finish; they are not allowed to use their hands or arms to hold the balloon during the race; the balloon must be carried by both of them during the race (i.e. not between one person's legs); and they must not allow the balloon to touch the ground during the race. If they break any of these rules, they are to come back to the starting line and start all over again.

9. Line the group up, and sing out: 'Go'.

10. After participants complete the race and there is a winner, you may award a prize.

Facilitator's notes

Sample debriefing questions

Which pair won?

What technique did they use?

What problems did each pair have?

Would more planning time have been of benefit?

How could it be done better if we had to do it again?

How does this activity relate to the workplace?

Safety issues

Observe everyone closely, as some people tend to watch the balloons instead of watching where they're going.

Ensure there is nothing for participants to trip over in the playing area.

Variations

1. This activity can be done in trios.

2. Planning time, say 2 minutes, can be included at the start of the activity.

Time required

As long as required. The briefing takes only a minute during the course, and the 'show' is usually presented during or after an evening dinner.

Size of group

The bigger the better.

Material required

None.

Overview

This activity is for use with large groups on courses that run over several days. It is usually conducted as an evening activity around the barbeque.

Goal

To develop a sense of team spirit.

Procedure

1. Tell the group that they will be having a barbeque one evening during the training program, and that a talent quest will be held during or after the meal.

2. Tell the group that you need volunteers to participate in this quest, and that participants can volunteer either solo or in groups. Anyone wanting to take part in the talent quest should advise you beforehand.

3. After the talent quest, all the audience should vote on which performance was the best. The winner, along with all other acts, should be given prizes.

Variations

Groups may be formed and
briefed that each is to perform a
2 minute act.

Facilitator's notes

Try to encourage everyone to participate in this.

Time required

15 to 30 minutes.

Size of group

12 or more—the more, the better.

Material required

1 blindfold for each pair.

2 lengths of rope about 10 metres (30 feet) long.

Plenty of newspapers, or lots of cardboard or plywood discs about 60 cm (2 feet) in diameter (the 'mines').

Overview

This team activity can be used indoors as well as outdoors. It allows team members to build trust and improve communication.

Goals

1. To build trust within the team.
2. To improve communication.
3. To energise the group.

Procedure

1. Select a suitable place, preferably a flat and level area to conduct this activity.

2. Should anyone not want to participate in this activity, use them as observers. With a larger group this exercise can become quite loud. That's an advantage, as it becomes confusing where the directions are coming from and to whom they are directed.

3. Ask everyone in the group to choose a partner.

4. Give one person in each pair a blindfold and ask them to put it on.

5. When participants' blindfolds are in place, lay the 2 pieces of rope on the ground parallel to each other and about 10 metres (30 feet) apart. They mark the beginning and end of the minefield.

6. Make the minefield by laying plenty of open sheets of newspaper (or the cardboard or plywood discs) on the ground between the 2 ropes—the more sheets of newspaper or discs, the better.

7. Get the blindfolded person's partner to take them behind the rope that marks the beginning of the minefield. The blindfolded person should stand just behind the rope, with their partner about 2 metres (6 feet) behind them.

8. Your briefing could be something like this:

Several days ago you were captured during an outback rebellion. One of you has been able to escape from the cell you were being held in. The problem is that the person who managed to get out doesn't know what's outside. It's the middle of the night and it's pitch black outside— just ask the people with the blindfolds on how dark it is! Outside there is a minefield that must be crossed to reach safety. There is no way around it. The person still trapped in the cell— that's the person without the blindfold—knows the exact layout of the minefield and the location of every mine in it. What the people without blindfolds have to do is give their partners verbal directions so they can cross the minefield. If they touch, or bump into, anyone else on the minefield they are to 'freeze' for 30 seconds. Obviously, should anyone touch any of the mines, it's all over for them. Sunrise isn't too far away and, as a result, the final part of the escape needs to be completed quickly. Once the sun comes up, the guards will be able to see anyone left in the minefield and they will be shot. It's time to go. Good luck.

Sample debriefing questions

Who was first to cross?

How did everyone feel about this exercise?

How clear were the communications?

What problems were there?

How does this activity relate to the workplace?

Safety issues

Keep a close watch on the blindfolded participants, obviously they cannot see where they are going.

Variations

1. This game can be played indoors by placing 2 long strips of masking tape at each end of a room and open sheets of newspaper on the floor between them. The strips of tape mark the start and finish of the minefield, and the sheets of newspaper represent the minefield.

2. The minefield can be covered with mouse traps, lego blocks or anything else that might represent mines.

Facilitator's notes

The trainer needs to be very observant with this exercise, both for safety issues and to see whether anyone touches the sheets of newspaper.

Time required

60 minutes depending on the size of the group.

Size of group

10 to 24 people.

Material required

10 or 12 lengths of 32 mm (1¼ inch) hardwood dowel or water pipe, each about 1 metre (3 feet) long.

Overview

This is an easy but powerful trust building activity that can be used during any team building program.

Goal

To develop a sense of trust between participants.

Procedure

1. Ask the group to form pairs. If you have one person left over, they will be the first climber. If you have even numbers, select one person in a pair as a climber and the other as a spotter.

2. Give all the remaining pairs a length of dowel (or water pipe). Ask all pairs to stand in a line, and then each pair to face one another. You should finish up with 2 lines of partners facing each other. Have each line stand shoulder to shoulder.

3. Show participants how to make a horizontal ladder, with each pair holding a rung of the ladder. Ask each pair to hold either end of their piece

of dowel (or water pipe). They need to hold their 'rung' tightly, somewhere between their waist and shoulders so that it is parallel with the ground. What they are doing is forming a horizontal ladder with a few bumps in it so, if they haven't done this already, maybe you could suggest that they hold them at different levels.

4. Take your designated climber to one end of the ladder and ask them to climb the ladder to the other end. Their task is complete when they get to the other end. If you only have a small number of pairs, say 4 or 5, have the first few pairs move to the other end of the ladder once the climber has passed over their 'rung'—then the ladder can be as long as you, or they, want it to be.

Sample debriefing questions

How did everyone feel before they started their climb?

How did everyone feel after they finished it?

How did you feel as you were climbing over the rungs?

How did the people holding them feel?

Safety issues

Make sure all sharp edges are taken off the dowel or pipe. Be certain everyone has a firm grip on their piece of dowel. This is a trust exercise so, if anyone falls, it will be difficult to rebuild trust.

Do not allow anyone to hold the dowel above shoulder height.

Variations

1. Have the line twist or change direction.

2. Have the climber wear a blindfold—but don't let the participants holding the dowels wear blindfolds!

Facilitator's notes

Time required

10 to 15 minutes.

Size of group

Unlimited, but very large groups need to be broken into smaller groups of 15 to 20 participants.

Material required (for each group)

3 tennis balls or small low-impact balls (low-impact balls are best).

Overview

Here is an activity designed so that everyone gets to know each other's name.

Goal

To be able to recall each other's names.

Procedure

1. Select a flat, level and clear area.

2. Ask the group to stand in a circle. Each participant should stand a good arm's length from the person beside them. You, as the facilitator, should stand in the circle with the group.

3. Tell the group that you are going to call out your own name and then pass the ball to the person on your left. When they get the ball, they are to call out their name and pass the ball to the person on their left, and so on.

4. Once the ball has gone around the group, tell participants there's now a new set of rules. This time you will call out someone else's name and throw the ball to them. When they catch it, or retrieve it, they will call out another person's name and throw the ball to them, and so on.

5. After a few minutes, when it appears that participants are starting to remember most of each other's names, take out a second ball and do the same thing with it.

6. Add a third ball towards the end just for fun.

7. Before breaking up the group, ask for volunteers to go around the group and name everyone correctly.

Safety issues

Make sure that people don't throw the ball too hard. Your initial demonstration should be a gentle lob.

Variations

1. If there is more than one group, rotate half of each group with another at various points during the activity.

2. You may also suggest that anyone can change groups at any time during the activity. All they have to do is leave their old group and walk up to another group but, to be accepted into the new group, they must call out their name so that someone can throw the ball to them.

Facilitator's notes

Time required

10 to 15 minutes.

Size of group

Unlimited if time permits. Normally used for groups of up to 24 participants.

Material required

None.

Overview

This is a simple activity/icebreaker that energises the group while building team spirit.

Goals

1. To liven up participants after lunch.

2. To get participants moving and laughing.

3. To increase team spirit through simple problem-solving.

Procedure

1. Ask the group to stand in a tight circle.

2. Ask all participants to raise their left hand in the air. Ask them to point their right hand towards the centre of the circle. When all participants have complied with your instructions, tell them to lower their left hand and grab someone else's right hand. Once this contact

is made they are not allowed to break it or to let go.

3. Tell participants that they are to untangle themselves without breaking their grip on each other. When untangled, they should again form a circle. Tell them not to worry if some participants are facing away from the centre of the circle at the completion of the exercise. It's possible with this activity that, rather than finishing up with one large circle of people, they may finish up with 2 or more smaller circles. If you don' t want this to happen, have the group perform a circuit test. To do this, after the group has completed step 2, select one person in the group. Ask them to tighten their grip with their right hand, effectively squeezing their partner's left hand. Once that person feels their left hand being squeezed, they are to pass this squeeze through to their right hand and so on. If you have one large group, the squeezes will work their way back to the first person you selected. If it didn't, you may want to start all over.

Sometimes it's worth it, sometimes it's not.

Sample debriefing questions

What problems did you encounter? How did you overcome them?

What roles did people take?

How does this activity relate to the workplace?

Safety issues

Tell participants that, if they are being twisted or pulled into a difficult position, they may break contact momentarily but must re-establish contact as soon as they are in a more comfortable position.

If participants are struggling, or not very agile, tell them they can maintain hand contact instead of a hand grip. This means they will be able to rotate their hand contact with their partner's and shouldn' t be forced into unusual positions.

Variations

Blindfold all, or half, of the participants. This will lead to other obvious points to cover in the debriefing.

Facilitator's notes

Time required

15 to 20 minutes.

Size of group

Unlimited, but the larger the group, the more balls needed.

Material required

7 or 8 tennis balls, or similar, for each participant.

Overview

Here is an activity that should have participants covered in perspiration at the end—that's from both laughing and running.

Goals

1. To energise the group.
2. To have participants work as a team.

Procedure

1. Select a large level surface to 'play' on. A sealed surface, such as a carpark or tennis court, would be good. You need to have one person to roll balls into the group and several observers to keep count.

2. Start by telling the group that they are going to be involved in a world record attempt. Tell them that the world

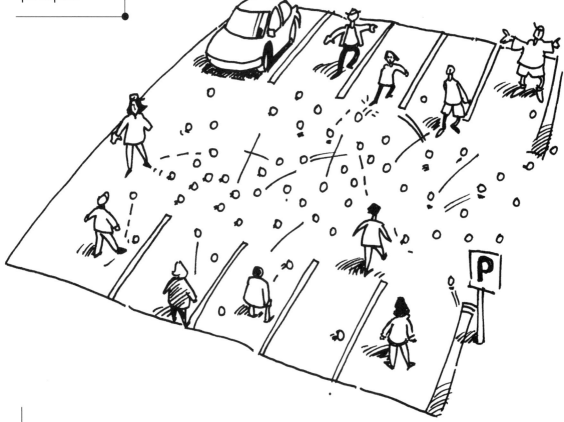

record for this activity is 5 balls per participant, so they should be aiming for a score at least 5 times the number of people involved.

3. What they have to do is keep as many tennis balls as possible moving on the ground. The balls must be rolling to be counted. They are not allowed to touch the balls with their hands, only with their feet. A ball must be kicked—not kept underfoot and moved back and forth— to stay in play.

4. The 'ball roller' is to keep rolling tennis balls into play for the group. The observers are to keep count of all balls in play (these are the balls the participants have managed to keep rolling).

5. Have participants spread out and start rolling the balls into the middle of the group one at a time.

6. When it appears that the group has achieved the maximum number, let them continue for another 30 or 40 seconds, then call a stop to the activity.

7. Ask the observers what the official count was, and congratulate the group.

Sample debriefing questions

What was the problem? How did you break it down? Who did what?

Did participants work as a team or as a group of individuals?

Would more planning time have been a benefit?

Safety issues

It's essential that people be asked to watch where they walk or run, particularly towards the end of the activity when balls are moving everywhere.

Variations

1. Allow the group to have a few minutes planning time after the initial briefing.

2. If there aren't enough balls, you can ask participants to keep them bouncing (instead of rolling). That should at least halve the number of balls required.

Facilitator's notes

15. Bouncing Beach Ball

Time required

10 to 15 minutes.

Size of group

Unlimited, but large groups need to be broken into smaller teams of 8 to 16 participants.

Material required

1 inflatable beach ball.

1 large playing field.

Overview

Here is an activity that will have everyone involved, even if they don't really want to be.

Goals

1. To develop a sense of teamwork.
2. To have the team work cooperatively.

Procedure

1. Ask the group to stand in a circle.

2. Tell them that you are going to ask them to challenge a previously set world record.

3. What they have to do is keep a beach ball in the air for more than 2 minutes and 16 seconds while hitting it

no less than 136 times. No one participant is allowed to hang on to the ball during this time. Participants must hit the ball into the air and keep it there only by hitting it repeatedly. The only other rule is that no participant is allowed to hit the ball twice in a row. This means that each participant must hit the ball to someone else.

4. If the group achieves this aim too easily, up the record. Tell them either that you misread the figures or you've just been advised that another group set a new world record earlier today.

Safety issues

Watch to ensure no one trips on anything, and make sure they don't bump into anything (like a tree). If play happens to move into any area you consider unsafe, have the group stop and restart play.

Variations

You can introduce a second, and perhaps third, ball so the group can set new world records.

Facilitator's notes

16. Pulse Speed

Time required

10 minutes.

Size of group

Unlimited—the bigger, the better.

Material required

A stopwatch (a standard piece of equipment for outdoor training).

Overview

Here is a quick and simple activity to get the team working together and having some fun.

Goals

1. To bond a team.
2. To have the team compete with itself.

Procedure

1. Start by asking the group to stand in a circle.

2. Ask everyone to hold hands.

3. Select one participant and ask them to squeeze the hand of the person standing on their right. Ask the second person if they felt the 'pulse'. Tell them that when they feel it next time, they are to squeeze the hand of the person on their right, and so on, until the pulse comes back to the starting point.

hmmm!

4. Tell the group that you are going to time the activity to see how fast they can do it. Start your stopwatch and tell them to go.

5. Let them know that the result wasn't too bad, but it can certainly be improved. Have them do it a second time, and let them know that they must have a faster time.

6. Repeat this for a few rounds, timing each attempt.

7. When they appear to be comfortable with this, have them reverse the direction of the pulse (that is, pass it to their left).

8. After several trials in the new direction, have the group revert to the original direction (to their right) but this time do it with their eyes closed, or have them all turn around so they are facing out.

9. At the end, and just for fun, have the first person send the pulse in both directions at the same time. Tell that person quietly so no one else knows what's happening. Watch the reaction of the participants on the other side of the circle!

Sample debriefing questions

Why did the group lose time when the direction was reversed?

Why did it take longer with their eyes closed?

How did the participants on the far side of the circle feel about the last pulse sent around?

Variations

Try other ways of sending a 'pulse'. For example, have participants tap each other on the back or whistle.

Facilitator's notes

Time required

1 hour plus.

Size of group

Unlimited, but large groups need to be broken into smaller teams of 5 participants.

Material required (for each team)

4 lengths of 200 mm (8 inch) diameter timber, each about 45 cm (18 inches) long. Treated pine fencing posts or old telephone poles would be good. Make sure that they are no smaller than 20 cm (8 inches) in diameter, otherwise they are too hard to roll on soft ground.

1 hardwood plank, 30 cm (12 inches) x 5 cm (2 inches) and about 4 metres (12 feet) long.

1 length of rope, about 12 mm (half an inch) in diameter and 6 metres (20 feet) long.

2 lengths of rope, to mark the starting and finishing lines.

Overview

This is another initiative problem for small teams to work with.

Goals

To have small teams work together on a problem-solving activity.

Procedure

1. Select a suitable area for this activity—not a hard smooth surface, otherwise the poles will roll too freely and participants will fall off them.

2. Have the group form teams of 5 participants.

3. Once they have formed teams, you can nominate a leader for each team. (If you select someone fairly reserved as the leader, for any activity, it may have a huge impact on their self-image.)

4. Take all teams to the starting line. Give each team their equipment: the 4 round posts, the plank and the rope.

5. Tell the teams their task is to cross an open area, using only the equipment provided, without touching the ground.

6. The briefing may be something like this:

Your team has been working in the corner of a factory on a secret project. One of your team members has noticed that a vat containing a new type of highly corrosive acid has a broken pipe at the base of it. The acid has obviously been leaking for some time, as there is a pool of acid about 10 metres (30 feet) wide between you and the doorway. You need to get out of the factory quickly as the acid is producing gases that are making it very hard to breath. You are unable to walk through the acid. If you touch it with any part of your body, it will dissolve you in a matter of seconds. The only equipment your team can find to help with the crossing are 4 round posts, one timber plank and one piece of rope. The posts have been treated and are resistant to the acid, but the plank and the rope aren't. If they touch the acid on the ground, even slightly, they will dissolve almost immediately. If anyone touches the acid, their team members must take them back to their original working area and place them under the special shower there. This is the only way to stop the effects of the acid. Once this is done, they will have to start the crossing again, but this time obviously be more careful. The same applies to the plank and the rope. If they touch the ground, they must be taken back immediately to the shower area. To be successful you must get all of your team members out of the factory safely. Good luck!

Sample debriefing questions

What was the problem?

How did you break it down?

Who did what?

Who took on what roles?

How effective was your leader?

Did everyone participate in solving the problem?

Do you think your team worked as well as it could have? Why?

What would you suggest to have the team work more effectively?

Safety issues

Make sure there are no sharp edges on the timbers.

Variations

If the team needs to be challenged even further, have the acid fumes affect the vision of 2 of the team members—in other words, select 2 people and ask them to do the activity wearing blindfolds.

Facilitator's notes

Time required

30 to 60 minutes.

Size of group

Unlimited.

Material required

10 marshmallows
(5 each of
2 different colours)
for each participant.

1 headband for
each participant
(there should be
even numbers of
headbands in each
of the same
2 colours as the
marshmallows).

1 whistle for the
facilitator (another
standard item of
equipment for
outdoor training).

Overview

This is one of the few activities
that is best conducted in a heavily
timbered area.

Goals

1. To have each team compete
    against each other.
2. To improve teamwork.

Preparation

Before the activity commences,
select a large playing area as the
battleground where the teams
compete. Ideally there should be
lots of cover for people to hide
behind. You can tie coloured
ribbons to tree trunks to indicate
the boundaries of the playing area.

Procedure

1. Keep aside a couple of
    participants to use as
    observers. Split the rest of the
    group into 2 teams. Each
    team should have equal
    numbers of different-sized
    participants and less agile
    participants.

2. Name the teams after the
    colours of the marshmallows.
    If you have purchased white
    and pink marshmallows, one
    group will be the White team
    and the other the Pink team.
    Give them their coloured
    headbands. Give each team
    member 5 marshmallows in
    their team's colour.

3. Show the whole group the boundaries of the playing area. Tell them that each team will start at opposite ends of the playing area. Their task is to have every member of their team reach the other end of the field before the other team does. The first team to achieve this objective will be allowed to eat any weapons they have left over.

4. Explain the rules. Once a team member reaches the other end of the playing field, they are in a safe area and cannot be challenged. If you are able to hit a member of the other team with one of your marshmallows, they are to remain in a state of suspended animation for at least 30 seconds. Participants are not allowed to throw their marshmallows so that they hit an opponent's head or neck. A team member may reuse marshmallows that fall to the ground, but only those of their team's colour. If anyone gets hit by 3 marshmallows during the game, they must go back to the starting point and restart the game. The game will not commence until you blow the whistle.

5. Once you have explained the rules, let the teams go to their designated starting points and give them 5 minutes to plan their strategies. Start the activity by blowing your whistle.

6. After the game is complete, you can give out extra marshmallows for participants to eat while the debriefing takes place.

Sample debriefing questions

What was the problem? How did you break it down? Who did what?

What roles did people take?

Did any leaders emerge?

How does this activity relate to the workplace?

Safety issues

Use the observers to keep an eye on participants, particularly from a safety point of view. There will be plenty of things for people to trip over. Have your observers also watch for 'foul' shots, i.e. above the shoulders. Anyone found shooting above the shoulders must be sent back to their starting line. Observers should also keep count of how many times the players are hit, and send back to the starting line anyone who is hit 3 times.

Variations

Low-impact balls, or similar, may be used instead of marshmallows. Ensure that nothing harder than a marshmallow is thrown.

Facilitator's notes

19. Polo Balloon

Time required

20 to 30 minutes.

Size of group

Up to 24 people.

Material required

1 foam sword (these can be purchased at toy stores or cut out of slabs of foam rubber) for each participant.

1 headband (there should be even numbers of headbands in each of 2 colours) for each participant.

Plenty of large balloons—not the small hard ones, but the larger kind.

1 large playing area.

1 whistle for yourself, plus whistles for any observers you use.

4 lengths of rope (to mark out the playing area if it isn't a basket ball or tennis court).

Overview

This activity is guaranteed to bring the pulse rate up. It's full-on.

Goals

1. To develop teamwork.
2. To energise the group.
3. To improve team spirit.

Preparation

Ideally, the playing area would be a basketball court or a tennis court without the net. However you can conduct this activity on a grassed area if you mark out the boundaries, i.e. by laying lengths of rope on the ground to form the 4 sides of the playing area.

Procedure

1. Keep aside a couple of participants to use as observers. Use the observers to ensure that there are no ' foul' shots and that no one uses their foam sword to hit another participant. Tell the observers that, if they see either of these, they should stop the game by blowing

their whistle and let you know immediately.

2. Split the rest of the group into 2 teams.

3. Name the teams after the colours of the headbands, e.g. the Red team and the Blue team. Give each team its headbands and ask them to put them on. Give everyone a foam sword.

4. Show all participants the playing area, and state the rules. The objective of this activity is to score the most points. A team will be awarded one point every time they get the balloon across their score line, which is the boundary behind the opposing team. Participants may only hit or touch the balloon with the foam swords. Anyone who touches the balloon with their hand or foot will be penalised one point. Under no circumstances is anyone allowed to hit another player. If this happens, their team will receive a 2-point penalty. The playing time will be a total of 10 minutes. There will be a half-time break, when the teams will change ends.

5. After you have explained the rules, toss a coin to decide which team starts at each end. Allow the teams 5 minutes to develop their strategy, then get the game under way by blowing your whistle.

Sample debriefing questions

What strategies did each team come up with?

Did these strategies work? Why?

Did any leaders emerge?

How can we improve teamwork?

Safety issues

Ensure that there are no 'foul' shots and that no one uses the foam swords to hit other participants.

Variations

1. Use 2 balloons.

2. This activity can be played in pairs rather than teams. Alternatively it can be started as a pair activity and then extended into a team activity.

Facilitator's notes

20. Step Right In

Time required

5 minutes.

Size of group

Unlimited.

Material required

None.

Overview

This is an impossible task to accomplish, but it's a lot of fun.

Goals

1. To energise the group.
2. To set a tone for the following activities.
3. To have participants interact physically without being self-conscious.

Procedure

1. Have everyone stand and form a tight circle (you included).
2. Ask everyone to put their arms around the shoulders of each person standing beside them.
3. Tell the group that you are going to ask them to do something that is extremely

difficult. The group will be asked to take 3 giant steps towards the middle of the circle. To be successful in the task, the circle needs to remain intact with everyone still standing.

4. Once everyone understands what's required, ask them all to take one giant step forward on the count of three. Give the group praise and encouragement.

5. Now ask them to take a second giant step on the count of three. Don't worry about giving any encouragement here because there will be too much laughter.

6. Ask the group to take a third giant step forward on the count of three. This usually results in the circle being broken and some participants may end up on the ground—they didn't achieve their goal, but the activity certainly created a lot of laughter.

Safety issues

Watch closely on the third step to make sure no one falls too hard.

Variations

1. If you have a very large group (40 or more), it would be better to break into smaller groups.

2. This can be done as a blindfolded activity.

Facilitator's notes

21. Dynamite

Time required

5 minutes.

Size of group

Unlimited.

Material required (for each team)

1 balloon.

Overview

This activity has no purpose apart from having some fun with any balloons that may be left over from another game.

Goal

To create a sense of team spirit.

Procedure

1. Ask everyone in the group to break into smaller teams of 3.
2. Give each team a balloon and ask them to inflate it—not to bursting point, but about 75% full of air.
3. Ask each team to form a very tight circle with everyone facing inwards.
4. Get them to place the balloon in the middle of the team and hold it at waist level.
5. Now have everyone move in closer so that the balloon is wedged between the 3 of them. Each participant should now remove their hands from the balloon. It shouldn' t fall.
6. Now tell the teams that, on the count of three, you want them all to squeeze together so tightly that they burst the balloon. Let them know that the first team to do this will be given something special at the next break.
7. Count to three and give the 'go' signal.
8. If any team is having a problem breaking their balloon (and that usually happens), ask the teams that have burst their balloons to go and help them.

Variations

1. Rather than teams of 3, this can be a very intimate activity if it's done in pairs.
2. To make the activity a bit more difficult, do it with teams of 4.
3. You can conduct this activity blindfolded and in complete silence. Ask everyone to put on a blindfold and remain completely silent. Ask everyone to form a team of 3 without speaking. Give each team a balloon, followed by the instructions above.
4. If people are in a swimming pool (for whatever reason), have them do this in the water.

Facilitator's notes

22. Recycle Ball

Time required

15 to 30 minutes depending on how many rounds are played.

Size of group

Unlimited but the bigger the group, the more garbage needed.

Material required

Lots and lots of light, dry garbage (e.g. plastic carry bags, screwed up newspaper, empty toilet roll holders, biscuit packets, magazines, pieces of string, old pieces of clothing, paper napkins, plastic bread wrappers, small cardboard boxes).

1 volleyball net.

1 stopwatch.

1 whistle.

3 small pieces of paper stapled together.

Overview

If you have a volleyball net and a pile of garbage ready for recycling, then you're set to go with this activity.

Goal

To set up a competitive exercise between 2 teams.

Preparation

1. On the stapled pieces of paper, write '120 seconds' on the front sheet, '140 seconds' on the second sheet and '160 seconds' on the third sheet.

2. Either set up the volleyball net beforehand, or have the group set it up.

Procedure

1. Tell the group that they are going to be the first to play a new game. It's a green activity, because it uses recycling materials.

2. Have the group break into 2 smaller teams of equal numbers, and have them move to opposite sides of the volleyball net.

3. Get all your garbage and put half on each side of the volleyball net.

4. The aim of this game is to have the least amount of garbage on your side of the net when time is up. You will start and finish the game by blowing your whistle. Participants must throw their garbage over the net—not under it or around it. Each player can only throw one piece of garbage at a time, not 2 or 3 together.

5. Tell the group it has been suggested that you, as the facilitator, might have a favourite side and, as a result, might be tempted to blow your whistle when their side is clear of garbage but before the game has run its full time. To overcome this, you have written the game time on a piece of paper which is in your pocket (you actually have 3 sheets stapled together to allow for 3 rounds). After you blow your whistle to stop the game, you can show them the time on the piece of paper.

6. Ask them to prepare their garbage, and blow your whistle to start the game.

7. Stop the game at the correct time and, if it's not obvious which is the winning team, do a quick count of the number of pieces remaining on each team's side of the court.

8. Ask the losing team if they would like to have a rematch. Repeat the activity, but this time use the time on the next piece of paper.

Sample debriefing questions

What were the main problems?

What strategies did each team have?

Safety issues

Watch to make sure that no one throws any dangerous objects over the net.

Variations

1. More than 3 rounds can be played.

2. You can blindfold several team members. This will lead to additional questions in the debriefing.

Facilitator's notes

Time required

1 hour plus.

Size of group

Unlimited, but large groups need to be broken into smaller teams of 8 to 10 participants.

Material required (for each team)

1 small camping tent (a small dome tent with a fly, or a 2-person tent with ropes and tent pegs, would be ideal).

1 hammer (if the tents have tent pegs).

1 first aid kit (for hammered fingers!).

1 blindfold for each participant.

Overview

This activity tends to create frustration for some participants, and show others how dominant they may be.

Goals

1. To demonstrate how people tend to take on specific roles.

2. To have a team work effectively.

Preparation

Make sure the tents aren't too large. They should be small but reasonably complex to assemble. Tents with ropes and/or flies are usually best. If they pack down into a small bag, that's even better. Keep the tents out of sight. No one should see them before the activity commences.

Procedure

1. Start by breaking the group into teams of about 8 to 10 participants. Allocate an observer for each team. Have each team move to a different area so that everyone has plenty of room to move.

2. Give everyone a blindfold and ask them to put it on.

3. When everyone has their blindfold in place, put a tent (still packed in its bag) in front of each team.

4. After the tents have been distributed, brief the teams or have each observer brief their team. You may want to use a briefing something like this:

Your team is on its way back from an overseas trip. The plane you were on was caught in a terrible storm earlier today and was badly damaged. The pilot suggested that you each get a parachute and jump. On the way out, one of you also grabbed a survival kit. This kit contains a small tent. It is now close to midnight. The storm activity is still close and, because of this, there is no moon. It's completely dark. Everyone is cold and exhausted. Your task is to now assemble the tent in complete darkness. The storm appears to be moving back this way, so the sooner the tent is up the better. Good luck!

5. After all teams have finished, or you decide to call it time, you can lead a discussion about issues such as communication, instructional techniques, conflict resolution, leadership issues, delegation, or just about anything else—this activity covers them all!

Sample debriefing questions

What was the problem? How did you break it down? Who did what?

What roles did people take?

Did everyone feel as though they were involved? Why?

Did anyone emerge as a leader?

How could this have been done better?

How does this activity relate to the workplace?

Safety issues

If tent pegs are used, watch to make sure no one hits their hand with the hammer or trips over pegs once they've been put in the ground. Also watch out for participants tripping over ropes, as they usually finish up everywhere!

Variations

1. If any one person in a team dominates the exercise, and you'd prefer they didn't, they can be struck down with a sudden bout of jungleitis. Jungleitis is a rare tropical disease that affects the vocal cords. Anyone with jungleitis is unable to speak!

2. Instead of telling each team that they have a tent to put up, simply put the bag in front of them (once they have their blindfolds on) and tell them there is something in front of them that they have to assemble. That way they also have to work out what it is.

Facilitator's notes

Time required

10 to 15 minutes.

Size of group

Unlimited, but large groups need to be broken into smaller teams of 12 to 16 participants.

Material required (for each team)

2 large hula hoops (get the largest diameter possible).

1 stopwatch.

1 whistle.

Overview

Here is a fun activity that can be used at any time, whatever the reason.

Goal

To develop a sense of team spirit and encouragement.

Procedure

1. Ask the group to form teams of 12 to 16.

2. Ask each team to form a circle, with everyone facing inwards, and hold hands.

3. When each team has created a circle, separate one pair of held hands and hang 2 hula hoops on the free arm of one of this pair. Ask the pair to hold hands again to complete the circle.

4. Now tell the team that they have to pass the 2 hula hoops

around the circle, each hula hoop in the opposite direction. The exercise is complete when the 2 hula hoops are back at the starting point.

5.   Blow your whistle to start the activity and start your stopwatch.

6.   After the first attempt, congratulate the group for achieving their goal, and tell them how long they took to do it. Now let them know that they will be doing it again, but you expect them to do it much faster. You can conduct this activity 4 or 5 times without anyone becoming bored with it. For each round, make sure that they know they have to do it faster.

Sample debriefing questions

What was the problem?

How did you break it down?

Did anyone emerge as a leader or as a coach?

What helped with the activity?

What made it harder?

Were realistic goals set?

Safety issues

If anyone is not physically capable of participating in this activity, use them as a timekeeper or as an observer. If you have used observers, have them stand reasonably close to the person with the hoop so that they can catch them should they fall.

Variations

1.   You may decide to let the teams have a one-minute planning session in between each round.

2.   Ask teams to set a time goal for themselves on each attempt.

Facilitator's notes

25. Catch What You Can

Time required

20 to 30 minutes.

Size of group

Unlimited, but large groups need to be broken into smaller groups of 20 to 30 participants.

Material required (for each participant)

1 throwable item (for example, a nerf ball or other type of low-impact ball, tennis ball, frisbee, towel with a knot in it, or screwed up piece of paper).

Overview

Here is an easily organised activity that has everyone competing with each other and themselves.

Goal

To have participants compete with themselves and each other.

Procedure

1. Start by asking everyone to collect a throwable item. Read the suggestions under 'Material required' to generate ideas.

2. When everyone has their item, ask the group to form a large circle with everyone facing inwards.

3. Ask for 3 volunteers to stand in the centre of the circle. They can leave their object on the ground to mark their position in the circle. Have the 3 volunteers stand, facing outwards, in the centre of the

large group and form a tight circle.

4. Tell the group that on the count of three, they are all to lob their items to the 3 volunteers in the middle of the circle. The volunteers' task is to catch as many of the objects as possible. All of the objects are to be lobbed simultaneously.

5. Count to three and call out 'lob'.

6. See who has caught the most objects. This will be a lot less than you expect—in a lot of cases it will be zero!

7. Ask your 3 volunteers to return to their places in the outer circle, and have 3 more people go into the centre and repeat the exercise. Keep going until everyone has had a turn catching the objects.

8. After everyone has had their first turn, suggest that they all do it again and try to beat their previous score as well as trying to set a new group record. Have as many rounds as necessary.

Safety issues

Ensure that the objects selected are safe to throw, i.e. they have no sharp edges, they are not too hard and they are unbreakable.

Variations

It's interesting to have the participants in the centre wear blindfolds. The same procedure can be used, or each group of 3 could be given 30 seconds planning time to work out how they, as a team, can catch the most items. This makes it a team exercise as opposed to an individual attempt.

Facilitator's notes

26. Rollin', Rollin', Rollin'

Time required

30 to 60 minutes depending on the size of the group.

Size of group

From 9 up to about 20 participants.

Material required

1 gymnasium or timber floored conference room with somewhere to tie a rope on the ceiling. This activity could also be conducted in a car park that has a large tree overhanging it.

1 strong rope to hang from the ceiling (a gymnasium may already have this in place).

1 trolley (described below).

1 empty tennis ball can or similar.

1 set of protective wear. This includes a helmet, gloves, knee guards and elbow guards.

Overview

If you have access to a gymnasium or a timber floored conference room with somewhere to tie a rope on the ceiling, then this activity could be for you.

Goals

1. To develop a team spirit.
2. To have participants unselfconsciously touching each other.
3. To improve teamwork.

Preparation

The trolley can be made quite easily. All you need is a piece of 20 mm ($^3/_4$ inch) plywood, about 45 cm (18 inches) square, with a strong ball-bearing swivel caster screwed firmly to each corner.

Procedure

1. Have the group form a circle in the centre of the floor (the rope should be hanging in the middle). Each participant should be about an arm's length from the person beside them.

2. Ask for a volunteer to come to the centre of the group. Ask them to put on the safety equipment and stand on the trolley. They will be the rider.

3. Stand the tennis ball can in the centre of the group.

4. When the rider is wearing the safety gear and standing on the trolley, have them grab onto the rope.

5. Tell the group that they have to knock the tennis ball can over. The rules are that they must stay in their current positions, that they may only knock over the can with the trolley, and that the rider must be on the trolley at the time.

6. Tell the rider that they are to try to stop the can being knocked over by the trolley. Explain that, if they start to fall, they should hold on to the rope firmly. They should then slide down the rope to a gentle stop rather than falling on the floor.

7. Have one participant from the circle get the trolley rolling by going into the circle, taking the trolley and rider back to where they were standing and then give them a push towards the can. Get them to repeat this until the trolley and rider knock the can over. Have the rider count how many times they are pushed before the can is knocked over. You may consider applying a time limit for each pusher.

Sample debriefing questions

How hard did the riders find it to miss the can?

What strategies worked best for the 'pushers'?

How did you develop these ideas or strategies?

Did any leaders emerge?

Safety issues

If this activity is done correctly, there is little chance the rider will fall off the trolley. However, as Murphy is always around, make sure the rider wears protective clothing. Even so, keep an eye out for 'pushers' who may get a bit carried away and try to have the trolley break the sound barrier.

Variations

After each push, have the participants in the circle take a half step backwards, making the circle larger each time. This will mean that it won't take too long for the rider to finish up on the floor.

Facilitator's notes

HARDER!

Time required

30 to 60 minutes depending on the size of the group.

Size of group

Unlimited.

Material required

2 soccer balls (under-inflate them so they don't go too far when kicked).

1 whistle.

Even numbers of blindfolds in each of 2 colours, enough of each colour for half the participants.

1 large playing field.

Overview

If you need an activity to develop trust and communication, look no further.

Goals

1.   To develop trust.
2.   To improve communication.
3.   To improve teamwork.

Preparation

It would be great if you can use a football field. If this isn't possible, place several items on the ground to mark out the 4 corners, the goal lines (at each end of the field) and the sidelines.

Procedure

1.   Keep aside 2 or 3 participants to use as observers. Observers can assist with the safety issues and also act as linespeople. Take everyone out to the centre of the playing field and have the group break into 2 even-sized teams.

2. Ask everyone in the team to choose a partner.

3. Once the participants have formed pairs, give each team a set of coloured blindfolds. Name the teams after the colours, e.g. the Yellow team and the Green team. Ask one participant in each pair to put on a blindfold, i.e. in each pair, one person can see and the other can't.

4. Tell participants the objective of the game. They will be playing a game of soccer with a bit of a twist. Only the blindfolded person in each pair is allowed to touch the ball. Their sighted partner will give them verbal directions about where to go and what to do.

5. Explain the rules. Every blindfolded person is to assume the 'bumper' position, i.e. bend their elbows and hold their hands and arms up, palms facing outwards at about face height. This will protect their upper body if they accidentally bump into anything. Sighted participants are not allowed to touch their blindfolded partners—only give them verbal directions. There will be no goalkeepers.

A goal is scored when a blindfolded player kicks the ball over their team's goal line. You will be the referee. When a player scores a goal, take the ball back to the centre of the field and recommence play. High kicks are not allowed, and the ball must remain on the ground at all times. Any high kick will result in the referee stopping play and putting the offender in the 'sin bin' for a predetermined period. If a player kicks the ball out of bounds, the referee will roll it back into play. There are no 'offside' rules. The game will be played in 2 halves of 10 minutes each, and the teams will change ends at half time.

6. Once participants understand the rules, toss a coin to decide which team starts at each end. Place both soccer balls in the centre of the field and blow your whistle. The extra ball is meant to create some initial confusion, but it also means that 2 games will be played at the same time.

Sightless Soccer

Sample debriefing questions

Who won?

What determined the winner? Was it the team with the highest score or the pair that were able to kick the most goals?

How did the blindfolded participants feel during the game?

How clear were the instructions sighted participants gave their blindfolded partners?

What could have made them better?

What ideas or suggestions can we take back to the workplace?

Safety issues

Ensure that all blindfolded players maintain the 'bumper' position.

Do not allow high kicks. If they happen, you can guarantee someone will get hurt.

Variations

1. At half-time you can have the partners change roles so that the blindfolded partner becomes the sighted partner and vice versa.

2. If you have a very large group, use 3 or perhaps 4 balls.

Facilitator's notes

28. Tuber

Time required

1 hour plus.

Size of group

Unlimited.

Material required

1 headband or armband for each participant (there should be even numbers of headbands or armbands in each of 2 colours (e.g. red and blue) to identify the teams).

2 blindfolds.

2 large tyre inner tubes, the bigger the better (e.g. truck tyre inner tubes).

1 large playing field.

1 whistle.

1 patch kit and pump will come in handy as you'll probably have the occasional puncture!

Overview

This activity will have participants running and breathing heavily.

Goals

1. To have participants compete in an activity.

2. To have participants working together in teams.

3. To have participants unselfconsciously touching each other.

Preparation

1. A football field is ideal for this activity. If a football field isn' t available, place several items on the ground to mark out the four corners and the goal lines (at each end of the field). There's no need to mark sidelines.

2. Under-inflate the inner tubes (so there's less chance of injury). Mark each inner tube

73

so that it matches the team's colour, i.e. one red and one blue. An easy way to do this is to tie coloured ribbon around each tube.

Procedure

1. Have everyone come on to the playing field.
2. Put the 2 inner tubes in the centre of the field.
3. Break the group into 2 teams of equal size.
4. Give each team their set of headbands or armbands, and ask them to put them on.
5. Explain the objective of the game, and the rules. Here is a brief you may want to use:

The purpose of this game is to win. To win you must score as many goals as possible in the allocated time. The game will have 4 quarters of 10 minutes each. There will be a 5-minute break between each quarter. To score a goal, you must get your team's inner tube over the designated goal line, which is the boundary behind the opposing team. The game will start by each team standing behind their opponent's goal line. I will ask for one team member from each team to volunteer to wear a blindfold.

Once you hear my whistle blow, the game commences. While the rest of the team stay behind the goal line, the blindfolded participant needs to find their way to their team's inner tube—that's the one marked with their team's colours. You are not allowed to take your blindfold off to see where you are going. Your team members will tell you where to go and how to get there. Once you touch your team's inner tube, you can remove your blindfold. Also, at this point, your fellow team members are allowed to run on to the field and start playing. The only way to move the inner tube is to kick it, push it with your foot or knee it. You are not allowed to touch it with your hands or arms. If you touch it with your hands or arms, the inner tube must remain stationary for 10 seconds without anyone touching it. There are no sidelines in this game. You may go as wide as you want but, to score, the inner tube must cross the goal line from the inside of the field. You should see that this game requires not only an attacking strategy but also a defensive strategy. You should try to stop your opponents from scoring with their inner tube. The only rule here is that you are not allowed to put your leg inside the tube to stop it from moving. When a goal is scored, I will stop play and you will take both inner tubes back to the centre of the field ready for a new start—i.e. all players return to behind their opponent's goal line and one team member is blindfolded.

6. Once players understand the brief, have both teams move back behind their goal line, and select and blindfold a volunteer. Blow your whistle to commence play.

Sample debriefing questions

What was the challenge? How did you break it down? Who did what?

What roles did people take?

Did any leaders emerge?

How did the blindfolded runners feel to start with?

What strategies did you employ? Did they work?

What can we do to improve our teamwork?

Safety issues

Cover the valves on the inner tubes with plenty of gaffer tape to prevent any injuries.

If there are any obstacles near the playing area, have the 2 blindfolded players assume the 'bumper' position. This is where they bend their elbows and hold their hands and arms up, palms facing outward at about face height. This will protect their upper body if they accidentally bump into anything.

Don't allow players to wear heavy boots, unless there's snow on the ground!

Variations

1. Allow one or 2 minutes for planning time before the start of play.

2. For larger groups, have more teams and more inner tubes.

Tuber

Facilitator's notes

Time required

I hour plus.

Size of group

Unlimited.

Material required

I dark night.

I powerful torch, preferably with a narrow beam of light.

I playing area with a 'home base' in the centre and 2 landmarks, each in opposite directions from the home base (the home base can be a cabin, car, shed or large tree; the 2 landmarks can be anything from a garbage bin to a house).

Overview

Here's a blast from the past. It's an adaptation of the children's game Hide and Seek but with a few modifications, the main modification being that it's played in the dark. This means it can be used on programs that run over several days.

Goals

1. To develop team spirit.

2. To have participants compete among themselves.

Procedure

1. Have the group assemble outside in the dark next to the home base. Giving the briefing outside allows time for everyone to start developing their night vision.

2. Once you have the group together, tell them what the activity is and what the rules are:

This activity is called Hide and Seek. It's similar but slightly different to a game you probably used to play as a child. I will select one person to be 'It'—remember as a child calling out 'You're "It"!'? I will give this person the torch, which is to remain turned off until I say. They then need to hide their face and count aloud slowly to 50—that should be easier now that you're grown up! While they're counting, everyone else has to go and hide. Once the person with the torch gets to 50, they turn on the torch and start looking around. To 'catch' someone, you must shine your torch on a person and call out their name. Anyone caught then goes to a designated area to wait for everyone else (point the area out to everyone). In the meantime, everyone who is hiding is to try to get back to home base safely. To do this you must first touch one of the 2 identified landmarks. These are located at opposite ends of the playing area (point them out). You then need to get back to the home base without being caught. Once back to home base, you need to touch it and call out 'Safe!'. Make sure you watch where you walk or run. It's dark and there might be objects laying around you can trip on. The game will end when everyone is back at home base or has been caught. The first person to get back to home base safely will be the next 'It'.

3. Select the first person to be 'It', give them the torch and ask them to start counting to 50.

Safety issues

The facilitator must know the area well for this activity—if not, don't use it.

Try to have people outside well before starting this activity so they get used to the dark.

Variations

Tell the person with the torch that's it's only allowed to be turned on for 5 seconds at a time, and must remain off for at least 5 seconds in between. If you use this rule, ensure the person who is 'It' counts out loud the 5 seconds when the torch is off, so everyone else knows when the torch is about to be turned back on.

Facilitator's notes

30. Human Machines

Time required

15 to 20 minutes depending on the number of teams.

Size of group

Unlimited, but ideally 8 to 12 participants in each team.

Material required

None.

Overview

In this exercise participants form teams and build a human machine.

Goals

1. To liven up the group after a long lunch break or to get them moving first thing in the morning.
2. To develop team spirit.

Procedure

1. Start by breaking the group into teams of about 8 to 12 participants.

2. Give the teams 5 minutes to design a human machine in which each team member is a component of the machine. All the human components must rely on each other for movement, i.e. one action leads to another.

3. At the end of the planning time, have each team demonstrate their human machine.

4. The whole group is to select the best machine.

Variations

1. After each team has demonstrated their design, you can join together all of the human machines.

2. Ask participants to plan their design without speaking.

3. Ask each team to design a machine based on names you have written on slips of paper beforehand. These machines could include a sausage-making machine, large clock, fire engine, bicycle, calculator, paddlewheel steamer, typewriter, coffee percolator and concrete mixer. As they demonstrate these 'machines', have the other participants guess what they are.

Facilitator's notes

Time required

5 to 10 minutes.

Size of group

Unlimited, but large groups may need to be broken into teams of 5 to 7 participants.

Material required

1 packet of toothpicks.

1 packet of Life Savers®.

Overview

A quick, competitive activity to help develop teamwork within groups.

Goals

1. To develop teamwork.
2. To energise the group.

Procedure

1. Advise the group that they are going to be involved in a competition.
2. Break a large group into teams of 5 to 7 participants.
3. Give each team member one toothpick.
4. Give each team one Life Saver®.
5. Tell each team to form a line (or circle).
6. Ask each person to put their toothpick in their mouth and keep it there until the end of the game.
7. Give the Life Saver® to the person at the beginning of the line (or circle). Ask them to slide the Life Saver® onto their toothpick.
8. Tell this participant that they have to pass the Life Saver® from one person to the next, until the Life Saver® reaches the end of the line (or circle).

They can only use the toothpicks to pass the Life Saver®—no hands allowed. If anyone drops the Life Saver®, they can only use the toothpicks to pick them up. Remind them that the toothpicks have to stay in their mouths!

9. The first team to complete the task wins a prize—maybe a fresh packet of Life Savers®.

Sample debriefing questions

Who finished first?

What helped with this exercise?

What problems did you encounter? How did you overcome them?

How does this exercise relate to the workplace?

Variations

1. You can base the teams on existing work teams.

2. You can repeat this exercise say 3 or 4 times with one or 2 minutes between each round. Use the time in between for the teams to discuss strategies, then time each round to demonstrate improved results.

Facilitator's notes

Time required

40 to 60 minutes.

Size of group

4 to 12 participants.

Material required

2 identical sets of 50 bricks or blocks, ideally painted different colours so that each pile contains a mix of colours (this adds to the confusion).

1 pair of gloves for each participant (to handle the bricks).

Overview

A relatively simple exercise where everyone can see the problems associated with one-way communication.

Goals

1. To observe one-way communication not working.

2. To observe how the same scenario works using two-way communication.

Preparation

Apart from painting the bricks, you need to set up the area beforehand. Set up one pile of bricks in some kind of elaborate pattern or object in a separate area so that participants can't see it. In another area, which is within hearing of the hidden bricks, stack the second pile of bricks randomly. A good way to hide the first pile of bricks is to hang a blanket between 2 trees.

Procedure

1. Start by asking for a volunteer. This is a non-threatening role—all the volunteer has to do is talk.

2. Put the volunteer in the same area as the hidden bricks. Try to ensure that they don't see the second set of bricks and that the other participants don't see where you have taken the volunteer.

3. Tell the volunteer that their task is to get the group to build a structure exactly the same as the one they have in front of them. Exactly the same number of bricks is in each area. Only one-way communication is allowed. This means the volunteer can give instructions to the other participants but the other participants can't say a word. You need to enforce this rule, as there is always someone who asks a question. Stop any communication immediately.

4. Hand out gloves to the other participants and ask them to follow the volunteer's instructions.

5. Ask the volunteer to start.

6. After the other participants have finished, and before they have a chance to look at what their structure should look like, ask them the following questions:

How did you feel about being on the receiving end of one-way communication?

What emotions did you feel?

How closely do you think your structure resembles the original structure?

Ask the person who gave the instructions the following questions.

Do you think your instructions were clear?

How did you feel during the exercise?

Do you think the group has achieved something that's close to what you were after?

7. Now have everyone look at both structures.

8. After the laughter, lead a discussion about issues such as communication, assumptions and instructional techniques.

9. You can see whether

participants learned anything by selecting another volunteer who uses the hidden pile of bricks to build a different pattern or object. (To save time, you may use an assistant to do this during the discussion.)

10. Repeat the exercise but this time allow two-way communication. This time the structures should be very similar in appearance.

Sample debriefing questions

Can we have good one-way communication?

What are the essentials for good communication?

Safety issues

Watch to make sure bricks don't fall on participants' toes.

Variations

Instead of bricks, use 2 sets of paper cut-out shapes that are a mix of colours. The 2 sets of shapes need to be identical.

Facilitator's notes

Time required

5 to 10 minutes.

Size of group

Unlimited.

Material required

1 length of rope with a sliding knot at one end (to form a lasso). The length of the rope will depend on the size of the group.

Overview

This is a great activity that you can use at the start of a program to encourage a sense of teamwork.

Goals

1. To develop team spirit.
2. To have participants interact physically without being self-conscious.

Procedure

1. Place the rope on the ground in front of you, and make a circle with the rope. The circle should be just large enough for everyone to stand inside it comfortably.

2. Ask everyone to stand beside you.

3. Tell participants their task is to get everyone inside the rope circle without touching it. The rules are that everyone must have both feet inside the circle and both feet on the ground.

4. Your briefing may go something like this:

I want you all to imagine this. We are going on a walking tour through a large chemical plant. We are halfway through the tour when someone notices something pouring out of a large vessel. You are suddenly surrounded by the liquid. A worker yells to you that the chemical on the floor is highly corrosive. If one drop touches your foot or your leg, it will be completely eaten away. The worker also tells you that there is a safe area just in front of you that has a drain running around the outside of it so that no chemicals are able to get into it. The drain looks like an ordinary piece of rope but it isn't. It's a highly sophisticated piece of equipment. The only problem is that it's very brittle so, if anyone touches it, it will break and be of no use to you. The chemicals have spread almost to where you're standing, so everyone had better get into the safe area immediately. Good luck!

5. Once the group is inside the rope circle, ask everyone to step outside it.

6. Then, while you keep talking, pull on the loose end of the rope to make the circle smaller in diameter. Tell the group that, although they've been able to get out of that area, they're now trapped in another part of the plant and the safety area is much smaller.

7. Ask the group to get back into the circle, following the same rules.

8. Again, when they have done this, ask everyone to step outside the circle. Again, while you keep talking, pull on the loose end of the rope to make the circle even smaller in diameter.

9. Keep repeating this until all participants need to squeeze into the circle and hold on to each other.

Sample debriefing questions

Did anyone feel uncomfortable with the exercise? Why?

How does everyone feel about their own personal space?

Do some cultures have different views?

How will this impact on the future activities we have planned?

Safety issues

Make sure no one jumps into the group or tries to balance themselves on someone else's shoulders.

Variations

1. You can have the group do this activity in complete silence.

2. This is a fun activity to do blindfolded. Have one sighted person tell other participants what to do.

Facilitator's notes

Time required

30 to 60 minutes depending on the number of participants

Size of group

Up to

30 participants.

Material required

1 large ball of wool or string

Overview

An exercise you can use to conclude a lengthy program.

Goals

1. To provide participants with a way to pass on final messages to the whole group.

2. To encourage future networking among participants.

Procedure

1. Ask the group to stand and form a tight circle. You should include yourself in the circle.

2. Explain to the group what you are all about to do. Hold the loose end of the ball of string in one hand and the rest of the ball in the other.

3. Tell the group your final comments. You may say what you received from the

program or what you hope to see happen as a result of the program. After you have said your bit, hold the loose end and throw the ball to a participant on the other side of the circle. The participant who catches the ball is to give their final message to the group and, while holding onto the string, throws the ball to someone on the other side of the circle. This process continues until all participants have had a chance to speak. At the end, the pattern formed by the wool or string should resemble a spider's web.

Facilitator's notes

This exercise is best used with program participants who have spent a lot of time together.

35. Kangaroo Races

Time required

5 to 10 minutes.

Size of group

Unlimited.

Material required

At least 1 balloon for every pair of participants.

2 lengths of rope (to mark the starting and finishing lines).

1 playing field.

Overview

A fun activity designed to liven up any group.

Goals

1. To energise the group.
2. To promote teamwork.

Procedure

1. Place the ropes parallel with each other and about 10 metres (30 feet) apart to mark either end of the playing area.

2. Start this activity by having everyone form pairs.

3. Give each pair a balloon.

4 Ask the participant in each pair who is holding the balloon to stand on the line at one end of the playing area, and ask their partner to stand on the line at the opposite end of the playing area.

5. Ask the participants with the balloons to place them between their knees. Tell them that, once their balloon is in place, they are not allowed to touch it with their hands.

6. Explain how the game works. Tell the participants with the balloons that, when you give the signal, they are to hop like a kangaroo across the field (keeping their balloons between their knees). When they cross the line at the opposite end of the playing area, they are to pass their balloon to their partner—again, without either of them touching the balloon with their hands. Once the switch has been made, their partner is to hop back to the starting line.

7. The first pair to complete the second leg, still with their inflated balloon between their knees, is the winner.

Sample debriefing questions

Who got back to the starting line first?

What made this exercise difficult?

What made it easier?

Variations

After running this activity once, you can allow one or 2 minutes planning time and then repeat the exercise. This will allow the partners to discuss what they did the first time and how they can improve on it. You can keep a record of all pairs' times.

Facilitator's notes

Time required

I hour depending on the number of participants.

Size of group

12 to 20 people.

Material required

1 platform between 1.5 and 1.8 metres (5 to 6 feet) high (if a platform is not available, use a ladder or a tree stump).

Overview

Here is an exercise that is used on almost every outdoor team building program. It has the advantage of looking scary but, if done properly, is in fact very safe.

Goals

1. To build trust within the team.

2. To have individuals challenge themselves.

3. To work as a team by helping each other.

Procedure

1. Before you start this activity, have everyone take off watches, rings, belts with large buckles, and any other sharp objects. Also ask everyone to empty their pockets.

2. Start by asking for 2 volunteers: one to be a Faller and the other to be the Fall Master. The Fall Master will be in control of the activity. Have both volunteers stand on top of the platform.

3. Get the rest of the group to form 2 lines in front of and at right angles to the platform, i.e. perpendicular to it. These participants will be the Catchers. Participants in each line should stand shoulder to shoulder, from the shortest to the tallest, and the 2 lines should face one another. Have each of these participants put their arms out straight in front of them with their palms facing up. Their arms are to be alternated and juxtaposed to form a secure landing area. Tell them that they are not to hold hands with the person across from them or to hold onto their arms or wrists. Let them know that if they try to hold hands there is a very real possibility that they may bump heads with the person standing opposite them.

4. Tell the Fall Master that their job is to make sure that each Faller falls correctly. They are to make sure each Faller lines up so that they fall directly in between the 2 lines of Catchers. Because each Faller has to fall backwards, they must stand with their back to the Catchers. The Fall Master is to make sure that each Faller holds on tightly to their trouser seams, or has their hands firmly in their pockets or places their hands firmly on the side of each thigh (this will stop their hands from flying about). The Fall Master needs to tell each Faller to remain rigid as they fall. If they bend their body, they may pierce the lines of Catchers with the concentrated weight around their backside—in other words, they will end up on the ground. The Fall Master must ensure that each Faller

has their head tilted back as a means of remaining rigid. The Fall Master should tell each Faller that they are to remain rigid after they have fallen so that they can be passed along the line of Catchers.

5   The Fall Master is also responsible for making sure that each line of Catchers is evenly distributed according to size and strength. They may need to rearrange the lines of participants to achieve this. The Fall Master must also make sure that the Catchers are ready and waiting for each Faller to fall.

6. Each Faller should let the Fall Master know when they are ready to go. The Fall Master then yells, 'Falling', and tells the Faller that they can go.

7. Once the Catchers at the head of the lines have caught the Faller, they pass them along to the other end of the lines.

8. The 2 Catchers at the ends of the lines are responsible for holding on to each Faller' s torso while they put their feet back on the ground.

9. The Faller now becomes a Catcher at the end of the line. The person closest to the platform now becomes the next Faller. The cycle continues until everyone has had at least one turn at each role. Don't forget to let the Fall Master swap with someone so that they also have a chance to be a Catcher and a Faller

10. If anyone doesn't want to participate as a Faller, do not force or trick them into doing it. We are trying for 100% participation, but there might be one or 2 people who really won't want to do this. Have them just climb to the top of the platform and look along the line. Once they have done that, they can either come back down (and go to the end of the line as if they had done it) or rethink their decision. That's all the participation that's required. Never force anyone.

11. So what are you doing if the Fall Master is now controlling everything? Place yourself as one of the second or third Catchers in the lines. That way if anything happens to go wrong you can either help catch the person, or at least slow down their fall. After the

first couple of falls, you can stand back and be a spotter. If anyone asks why you're not participating, or suggests that you don't trust them to catch you, it's time for you to hop up and take your turn along with the rest of them.

Sample debriefing questions

What did you feel initially about the activity?

How do you feel now that you have attempted it?

How did you feel while standing on the platform?

Safety issues

Under no circumstance should participants fall further than 1.8 metres (6 feet). Otherwise, the Faller's head and shoulders may reach the Catchers before the rest of their body does. If this happens, it's very easy for the Catchers to drop the Faller because all their weight is concentrated in one area. If the Faller's head and shoulders reach the Catchers before the rest of their body, they will be literally falling on their head, which would be extremely dangerous.

Have as many spotters as necessary. The number will depend on the type of group you have.

Ensure that Catchers have removed all watches, rings and other sharp objects. Ensure that each Faller empties their pockets and removes their belt if it has a large buckle.

Variations

For established teams, you may consider blindfolding the fallers.

Facilitator's notes

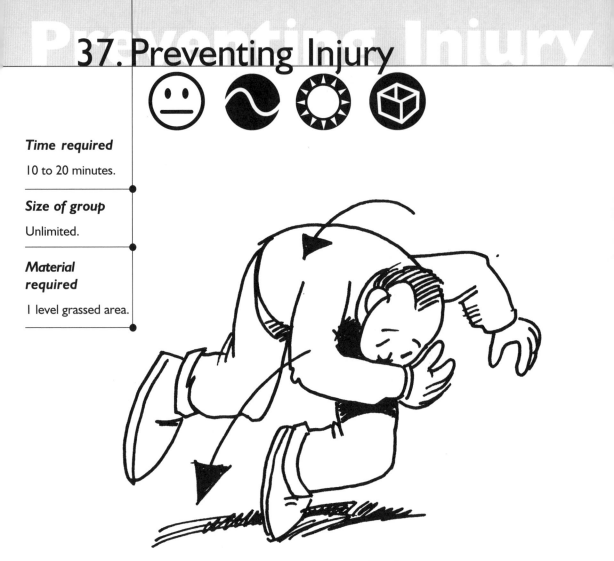

Time required

10 to 20 minutes.

Size of group

Unlimited.

Material required

1 level grassed area.

Goals

1. To explain the purpose of using a spotter.

2. To show participants how to fall correctly.

Overview

There are times when the difference between having fun and getting an injury is having a spotter close by or having participants know how to fall correctly. This activity should be used near the start of any program where spotters will be used or where participants need to know how to fall.

Procedure

1. Tell the group that there may be occasions on the program when the difference between having fun and being injured is simply a matter of having a good

spotter or knowing how to fall correctly.

2. Explain to the group what a spotter's main role is. A spotter's main role is to closely watch other participants in any activity, so the spotter can give them some protection should they happen to fall. There's no point in a spotter trying to catch the full weight of someone who is falling, as both participants could end up with more than a few bruises. The spotter's first priority is to protect the participant's head and upper body by offering physical support.

3. Let participants know that there are right and wrong ways to fall. The wrong way hurts, and the right way doesn't. Tell participants: ' Those who don't mind pain can go and have a cup of coffee. For those who are less inclined to feel pain, listen in' .

4. Tell participants that there are 2 types of basic rolls, a front roll and a back roll.

5. Explain front rolls. Your explanation could go something like this:

The front roll goes like this. You can do this from any position, including standing or squatting. If you want to roll forward on your right shoulder, start by tilting your right shoulder forward. Use your left arm as a guide but not as a brace. Place your right arm diagonally across your body with the palm facing in towards your left knee. Hold your right arm out at about a 45 degree angle from your body. Bend your right elbow slightly so that your right forearm can provide a surface for the beginning of the roll. You should also be looking under your left arm to make certain your head is in the correct position—that is, looking down and to the left. You then continue rolling forward onto your right shoulder in the tuck position, and finally into a squat position. Your roll will be at a 45 degree angle rather than straight ahead.

6. After the explanation, you need to give a demonstration (yes, you need to know how to do it!).

7. Have each person try it, one at a time, from a standing position so you can see any errors.

8. Repeat the procedure, but this time have each participant roll forward on their left shoulder. Reverse the above instructions.

9. Explain back rolls. Your explanation could go something like this:

Start from a standing position. Your legs should begin to bend as you turn your body slightly towards the hip that is going to first make contact with the ground. You will roll on the shoulder that is on the same side as the hip that made first contact. Use your hands to guide your tucked body as you complete the roll over your shoulder.

10. Again, after your explanation, give a demonstration.

11. Have each person try a back roll once from a standing position so you can see any errors.

12. Then ask participants to form pairs. Have them practise front and back rolls from a standing position, a walking position and a jogging position.

Safety issues

You may occasionally find that some people will not participate in this activity. If that's the case, they will not be able to participate in any following activity where there is a risk of falling. Instead, you can use them as spotters for any of the following activities in the program. Some people have fears about hurting themselves, and some people have physical limitations. Never force anyone to do anything they don't want to do. If you can, give them another role—such as helping to prepare for the next tea break—so that they are still involved.

Facilitator's notes

Time required

1 hour plus.

Size of group

Unlimited, but larger groups need to be broken into smaller teams of 5 or 6 participants.

Material required

None supplied—participants have to find their own!

Overview

Remember, back in your younger days, trying to build a homemade kite? This is just as much fun!

Goals

1. To have the team work on a problem-solving activity.

2. To have the team work in a cooperative manner to achieve a common goal.

3. To develop a sense of team spirit.

Procedure

1. Break a larger group into teams of 5 or 6 participants, and tell them their task.

2. Each team is to build a kite from materials team members can find.

3. Give participants 30 minutes to complete their task. After they have made their kites, they should test them to make sure they do in fact fly.

4. You can give them a briefing that goes something like this:

Your team has been shipwrecked on a small, deserted island. It has been several days now, and everyone is concerned about being rescued. One of you has just noticed a ship on the horizon. Assuming that someone is looking this way, there is no way that anyone would see you on the shore. You have no matches or other signalling devices. Your only hope is to build a kite. It's estimated that, if you can get the kite into the air within 30 minutes, there's every chance that someone on the ship will see it. You must find all of the materials to construct the kite. There are absolutely no supplies left in the wreck. Your 30 minutes is slipping away, so good luck!

Sample debriefing questions

Which teams managed to get their kites into the air within the 30 minute time limit?

What was the problem? How did you break it down? Who did what?

What roles did participants take?

How did participants feel about working to a fixed deadline?

Did the team work effectively? Why?

How could this have been better conducted?

Variations

Depending on the skill level of the group and the resources that may or may not be lying around, you can supply some materials for the teams to use. This can be made a very challenging exercise for the teams.

Facilitator's notes

Time required

I hour plus.

Size of group

8 to 12 participants.

Material required

1 blindfold for each participant.

1 bush track, between 200 metres (60 feet) and 1 km ($\frac{1}{2}$ mile) long.

Overview

This activity is great for building trust within a team. It's best conducted in an isolated bush setting to allow participants to listen to the natural bush sounds.

Goal

To build trust within a team.

Preparation

Try to choose a bush track in an isolated area where there are lots of birds and trees. You can make this activity more interesting by including a few obstacles, e.g. a fallen tree branch or a dry watercourse (but make sure the banks are not too steep).

Procedure

1. If necessary, request assistants to volunteer to help prepare the meal and to act as spotters.

2. Ask everyone in the team to put on their blindfold. Tell them that they must keep their blindfolds in place until the end of the exercise. Also let them know that you will

be with them the whole time and will act as a spotter should they find themselves in a difficult situation.

3. Once participants have their blindfolds are in place, give them a briefing something like this:

Your team is part of an expedition to the ancient city of Sound. Your research has led you to a person who is able to guide you to the remains of the lost city. It lies deep in an isolated jungle. You have been able to convince the guide, through an interpreter, how important your expedition is, and the guide has agreed to take you there. It is claimed that there are many gold coins and precious jewels still scattered on the ground throughout the city. It is also claimed that, if any of these coins or jewels are removed from the city, a curse will be put on the people throughout the land. Because of this, your guide will take you there, but only on the condition that you all wear blindfolds so you can't find your way back by yourself later. Because the guide doesn't trust the person that you used as an interpreter, the interpreter will not be going with you. Your guide doesn't speak your language, so they can' t

communicate with you verbally. They may, however, make other sounds or noises that you will have to interpret. Your guide will be here in a couple of minutes, so please prepare yourself to travel safely as a group. Do you have any questions?

4. Once you have briefed participants and dealt with all their questions, tap one participant on the shoulder, and ask them to take their blindfold off and come with you. Take them out of earshot and tell them that their role is to be the group's guide. They are to lead the group safely to their destination (tell them where that is). They are not allowed to speak but they can whistle, clap their hands or do anything else they can think of to communicate. They may only touch one person at a time, and only by hand.

5. Take the guide back to the group, and tell the group that their guide is ready. Several things can happen here, so be prepared.

6. At the end of the walk, have everything ready for a coffee

or lunch break. If you have enough assistants, and one of them can be sent out earlier, a barbeque is a great idea. After the break, take participants back along the walk so that they can see where they walked and whether they can locate the source of the sounds they heard.

Sample debriefing questions

How did everyone feel during the walk?

What sounds did you hear?

Did you trust your leader, the guide?

How did those at the back of the line feel?

Did your trust levels increase or decrease as time went by?

Safety issues

It's a good idea to have at least 2 spotters on this activity. They need to remain alert at all times. In this activity, participants tend to be incredibly trusting of their leader, and they'd walk straight over the edge of a cliff if their guide led them there!

Variations

Tell the guide that they are not allowed to touch anyone during the activity. You could explain this in your brief by saying it had something to do with religious beliefs or health reasons. Be creative!

Facilitator's notes

Time required

5 to 10 minutes.

Size of group

Unlimited.

Material required

1 piece of plywood about 45 cm (18 inches) square.

1 roll of masking tape.

1 balloon (plus a few spares).

1 marking pen.

1 newspaper.

Overview

A simple activity designed to promote lateral thinking.

Goals

1. To get participants to think laterally.
2. To have the group participate in a problem-solving exercise.

Preparation

Before starting this activity, place a cross in the middle of the piece of plywood using two bits of masking tape, each about 30 cm (12 inches) long.

Procedure

1. Start this exercise by asking for a volunteer. Tell the volunteer that they are going to be asked to solve a problem. The problem will be to retrieve a balloon from the ground using the materials supplied.

2. While you are talking, blow up the balloon. It can add

some fun to write on it something like 'extremely valuable' or '$$$', or to put a few lollies inside the balloon as a reward for retrieving it (they also help prevent the balloon from blowing away!).

3. Place the piece of plywood (with the cross facing upwards) on the ground so that everyone can see it.

4. Ask the volunteer to stand in the middle of the cross. Give them the newspaper. Place the balloon on the ground about 4 metres (12 feet) away from the edge of the piece of plywood.

5. Ask the volunteer to retrieve the balloon without moving from the cross. They have 3 minutes to complete this task. The rest of the group is to observe only—they are not to offer suggestions about how to solve the problem.

6. After 3 minutes, assuming that your volunteer hasn' t completed the task, ask the group for suggestions about how to solve the problem.

7. You can then lead into a discussion about issues such as problem-solving, synergy and teamwork.

Sample debriefing questions

What was the problem?

How did you break it down? Who did what?

How many participants could see an answer to the problem?

How many ways are there to solve this problem?

What rules do we tend to place on ourselves?

Variations

Once the volunteer is standing on the plywood, have them put on a blindfold and have the group tell them what they have to do. This will obviously lead to other issues in the debriefing.

Alternatively, do this as a small group exercise. Use a 1 metre (3 feet) square piece of plywood instead, and have all the small group stand on it. Their task is to retrieve the balloon, using the same rules.

Solution

Here's one solution. Roll the newspaper up fairly tightly, then gradually pull the inside of it out from one end to lengthen the roll and create a pole. Tear a piece off the masking tape that's on the plywood. Put this piece of tape on the end of your pole so that some of the sticky side remains exposed. All you need to do then to retrieve the balloon is to touch it with the sticky end of your pole!

Facilitator's notes

Time required

15 to 20 minutes depending on the size of the group.

Size of group

8 to 16 participants.

Material required

1 blindfold.

1 solid wall (use the side of a building or perhaps a row of cars).

Overview

This is a simple trust building activity.

Goal

To have participants increase their trust level in each other.

Procedure

1. Select a flat and level area with no hidden obstacles in the grass that the blindfolded volunteer can trip on.

2. Start by having the group line up against the wall (or some other solid object).

Participants should stand a good arm's length from one another.

3. Ask for 2 volunteers. Ask one of them to put on a blindfold.

4. Explain the exercise. Tell the sighted volunteer that they will take their blindfolded partner about 10 metres (30 feet) away from the wall, then make sure they're facing the middle of the group of participants that are lined up along the wall. The sighted volunteer is now to let go of the blindfolded volunteer.

5. The blindfolded volunteer needs to assume the 'bumper' position. This is where they bend their elbows and hold their hands and arms up, palms facing outward at about face height. This will protect their upper body if they accidentally bump into anything.

6. The group that is lined up along the wall needs to be completely silent and still. Their job, apart from remaining silent and stationary, is to stop the blindfolded person from bumping into the wall—in other words, as the blindfolded person gets to

the line, they should 'catch' them so that they don't touch the wall.

7. The blindfolded volunteer's partner is to act as a spotter while they move. They shouldn't be too close but close enough to catch the blindfolded volunteer should they happen to trip on anything. The spotter is also to remain totally silent. When everything is ready, tell the blindfolded person to walk at a brisk pace or jog towards the wall while maintaining the 'bumper' position.

8. Once the group has 'caught' the first blindfolded volunteer, have participants change roles so that everyone gets to experience being blindfolded and acting as the blindfolded person's spotter.

9. Repeat the activity a second time.

Sample debriefing questions

How did everyone feel about walking blindfolded?

Did everyone feel more comfortable doing it the second time? Why?

How did the spotters feel about their role?

How can we be more supportive of our team members in the workplace?

What stops us from doing this at present? How can we overcome this?

Safety issues

Make sure each walker maintains the 'bumper' position and that their spotter is vigilant.

Variations

Have 2 blindfolded volunteers walk to the wall simultaneously, so that they race to get to the wall first. You can do this after everyone has had their first turn, instead of repeating the activity the same way a second time.

Facilitator's notes

42. All Tied Up

Time required

20 to 40 minutes depending on the size of the group.

Size of group

8 to 20 participants.

Material required (for each team)

1 rope about 30 metres (110 feet) long (long enough to tie around the group about 5 times).

1 walking trail, about 100 metres (300 feet) long, depending on the difficulty of the obstacles.

Overview

This is an icebreaker that encourages participants to get to know each other a little better.

Goals

1. To involve participants in a group initiative.

2. To have participants learn something about their fellow team members.

3. To have participants interact physically without being self-conscious.

Preparation

Select a trail, which you can mark out beforehand using coloured pieces of ribbon tied to tree trunks and low branches. It makes it more interesting if they have to overcome a couple of obstacles along the way, e.g. a fallen tree or a couple of steps on a stairway.

Procedure

1. Ask the group to form a tight huddle. Everyone needs to be in nice and close.

2. Wrap your length of rope around the whole group. Make about 5 turns around the group, keeping the rope tight but not so tight that it stops them from moving (or breathing!). When you have used all the rope, tie it off.

3. The group's task is to follow the trail that you point out.

4. While they are moving along the trail, you will ask each person in the group to disclose something unusual about themselves, as well as something they are proud of doing or having been involved with. Tell the group that, when they reach the end of the trail, you will ask participants at random to repeat what others have disclosed, so they'd better listen attentively.

Sample debriefing questions

What did you find out about other people that you didn't already know?

How do you think the group handled the initiative?

Safety issues

Keep a close eye on everyone to make sure they don't trip on anything and fall. If one participant does fall, it will probably bring down the whole group and the rope may hurt.

Variations

1. If there isn't time to mark out the trail beforehand, you can explain the trail verbally or you can just walk in front of the group and have them follow you.

2. If you really want to challenge the group, have them do this activity blindfolded. Have a couple of spotters handy.

Facilitator's notes

43. Pick A Box

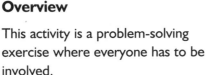

Time required

5 to 15 minutes depending on the size of the group.

Size of group

Up to 24 participants.

Material required

1 piece of plywood for each participant plus 1 additional piece. Each piece should be about 30 cm (12 inches) square.

Overview

This activity is a problem-solving exercise where everyone has to be involved.

Goal

To have the team participate in a problem-solving activity.

Preparation

Place the plywood squares on the ground in a straight line with about a 30 cm (12 inch) gap between each square.

Procedure

1. Have the group break into 2 teams of equal size. If there's an odd number of participants, have one person assist you.

2. Ask one team to stand on the squares to the left of the line, one team member in each square. Ask the other team to stand on the squares to the right of the line, one team member in each square. Both teams face the middle square, which has no one standing on it.

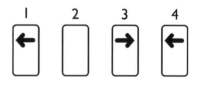

3. In the above example, there are 16 participants—that is, 8 in each team—and an empty square in the centre. A team member stands in each square that contains an arrow. The arrows show which way the participants face—that is, the teams face one another.

4. Each team's task is to get from the squares on their side of the line to the squares on the other side, using the following rules.

5. Here are the rules. No one is allowed to turn their body around. You may look behind you, but your body must continue to face the direction it was in to start with. Each team can take only one turn at a time—that is, only one team member can move at each turn.

6. You can move into an empty square in front of you. In example 1, the person in square 1 or the person in

square 3 can move into square 2.

7. You can also move past an opposing team member to the square in front of them, but you cannot move backwards. In example 2, the person in square 4 can move into square 2 but the person in square 1 cannot move into square 2.

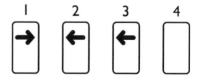

Example 2

8. You are not allowed to pass anyone facing the same way as you, i.e. if you can see the back of their head. You are not allowed to pass 2 opposing team members to the square in front of them. In example 3, no one can move.

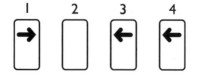

Example 3

Example 1

9. If you find yourself in a position where no other moves are possible, everyone must go back to their original starting position and try again.

Sample debriefing questions

What was the problem? How did you break it down? Who did what?

Who became the team leader?

Did the team work effectively at solving this problem?

How could you do it better?

Variations

If this is a one-off activity, instead of the plywood squares, you can use sheets of newspaper or draw chalk squares on the ground. They work just as well.

Facilitator's notes

Time required

I hour plus.

Size of group

8 to 12 participants.

Material required

3 dead tree trunks or lengths of timber about 5 cm (2 inches) to 7.5 cm (3 inches) in diameter, 2 of which should be about 4 metres (12 feet) long and the other I about 2 metres (6 feet) long.

3 pieces of rope, each about I metre (3 feet) long (enough rope to tie the 3 trunks together).

6 lengths of rope, each about 6 metres (20 feet) long.

Overview

This is an interesting challenge that uses readily available materials. Participants will build it and use it!

Goal

To have participants work as a team to solve a problem.

Procedure

1. Start by getting the team together.

2. Give participants the 3 tree trunks and the 3 short pieces of rope. Their first task is to build a structure that looks like the letter 'A'. Tell them that the crossbar on the letter 'A' must be strong enough for someone to stand on it.

3. Get participants involved in the second part of the activity, in which they have to stand the structure upright and have someone stand on

the crossbar. To help support the frame, they are allowed to tie the other 6 ropes onto it. No one else, apart from the person standing on it, is allowed to touch the frame.

4. Ask participants to move the frame a distance of 30 metres (100 feet). They must do this with the person still standing on the crossbar but with no one else allowed to touch the frame. Also tell them that at least one point of the frame needs to be in contact with the ground during the activity, and that no one is allowed to get any closer than 3 metres (10 feet) to the frame itself. Tie a coloured ribbon to each of the ropes 3 metres from the frame, so participants can easily recognise this limit.

5. Your brief can go something like this:

Your team has been on an expedition into the deepest jungles of Hotspot. While in the jungle, one of your team-mates contracted a rare disease. This disease is highly contagious and you must remain at least 3 metres (10 feet) away from the person at all times. To get your team-mate to safety, you must arrange for them to cross a narrow strip of land.

This area is approximately 30 metres (100 feet) wide. The problem here is that the grass growing on this strip of land has an undesirable effect on anyone with this disease. It is to be avoided at all costs. The result of this person touching the grass is indescribable. Your group has decided to build a structure using 3 tree trunks that have been found in the area. You can lash them together with the 3 short pieces of 'rope vine' you have been able to locate. To help your team member cross the grassed area, you have also agreed to tie the 6 pieces of 'rope grass' onto the frame to support it and stop it from falling over. It will also allow you to keep a safe distance from it. No other materials have been located, so this is all you have to work with. Good luck!

Sample debriefing questions

How did the team feel about this activity?

How did the 'diseased' team member feel?

Was the problem dealt with in a satisfactory manner?

Did the group behave like a team?

Safety issues

Make sure there are no sharp edges on the timbers and that they are strong enough to hold the weight of a person.

Variations

If you have a large group, break them into teams of 8 to 12 participants and give each team the challenge as a competitive exercise. Make it a race to cross the field.

Facilitator's notes

45. Quadripede

Time required

10 to 15 minutes.

Size of group

Unlimited, but large groups need to be broken into smaller teams of 7 participants.

Material required

2 lengths of rope (to mark the starting and finishing lines).

1 whistle.

Overview

You know what a centipede is—well, this is a quadripede. It's an extremely unusual animal with 4 legs.

Goals

1. To have a small group working together as a team.

2. To have participants interact physically without being self-conscious.

Procedure

1. Lay the ropes parallel with each other and about 10 metres (30 feet) apart.

2. Break the large group into teams of 7 participants.

3. Once participants have formed teams, take everyone over to the side of the field behind the starting line.

4. Tell the teams what they have to do. Their task is to

cross the field as a team of 7 participants. The rules are that the team has to remain together, team members must be in direct physical contact and the team may not use anything to assist them. The other important rule is that each team is allowed to have only 4 contact points on the ground at any one time. These contact points can be feet, hands, knees, backsides. If they have more than 4 contact points on the ground during the activity, they must go back and start again.

5. Let participants know that this will be a competitive exercise—in other words, a race with the other teams.

6. Give the teams 10 minutes planning time. Suggest that the teams move away from each other during the planning time so that other teams don't overhear their strategies.

7. Advise the teams that there will be 2 whistle blasts, the first warning that the race will start in one minute and the second indicating the start of the race.

Sample debriefing questions

What strategies did each team develop?

Did anyone feel this was unachievable initially?

How does everyone feel now?

Did the participants work as a team?

How could it have worked better?

Safety issues

Ensure people use correct lifting techniques during the activity.

Variations

1. You may wish to reduce the groups down to 6 in size in some cases.

2. Increase the distance between the starting and finishing lines.

3. Blindfold one or 2 participants in each team.

Facilitator's notes

Time required

10 minutes at the start of the program and 20 minutes at the end.

Size of group

Unlimited.

Material required (for each participant)

1 prepared Learning Support Contract.

1 pen.

Overview

This will help increase participant/supervisor accountability of learning back in the workplace. It will also give you feedback after the participant has gone back to work.

Goals

1. To have participants identify their training objectives before they start the program.

2. To have participants identify what they've learned during the program.

3. To have participants identify what they will do differently as the result of attending the program.

Procedure

1. At the beginning of the program, give each participant a copy of the

Learning Support Contract and a pen.

2. Ask participants to fill in parts 1 and 2 of their Learning Support Contract and then put it away for the time being. If participants fill in the Learning Support Contract before the program commences, have their supervisors agree with the objectives and sign if off.

3. At the completion of the program, ask participants to fill in parts 3 and 4 of their contract.

4. Ask participants to take their contracts back to work, discuss them with their immediate supervisor and together fill in part 5.

5. After each participant and their supervisor complete part 5, they are to make a copy of the contract and send it back to you.

6. You can then read through the information and, if relevant, attach this copy to the participant's personal file or similar.

Variations

1. After participants complete parts 1 and 2 of the contract, you can ask them to share their objectives with the group.

2. After participants complete parts 1 and 2 of the contract, you can ask each participant to choose a partner and discuss their objectives with one another.

3. Participants can complete parts 1 and 2 before they attend the program.

Facilitator's notes

Learning Support Contract

fold here when finished

Please return completed copy to:

_____

_____

_____

_____

_____

staple here   staple here

Part 1   **Learning Support Contract**

       Participant's Name: _____

       Program Attended: _____

       Telephone Number: _____

Part 2

       Workshop Objectives

       Write down your objectives for attending this program:

       1. _____
       _____
       2. _____
       _____
       3. _____
       _____
       4. _____
       _____
       5. _____
       _____
       6. _____
       _____

       Signed: _____ Participant

       _____ Participant's Supervisor

Part 3

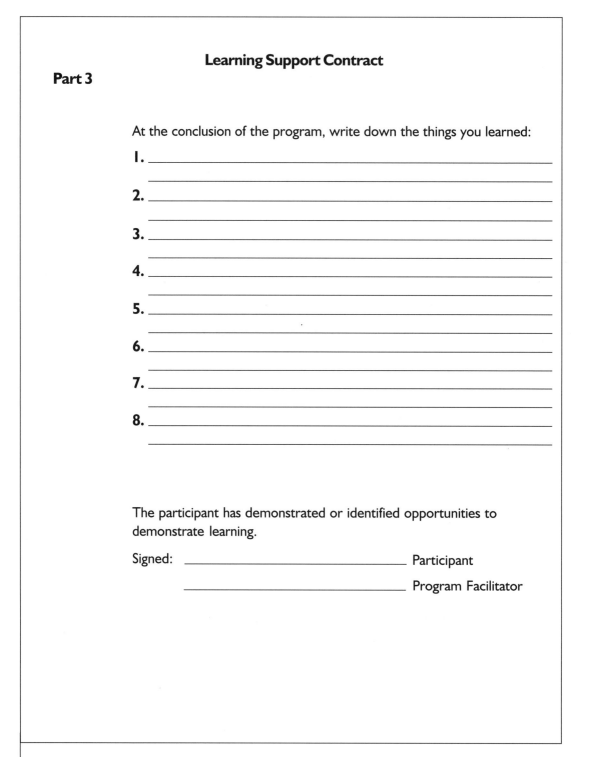

Learning Support Contract

At the conclusion of the program, write down the things you learned:

1. _____
_____

2. _____
_____

3. _____
_____

4. _____
_____

5. _____
_____

6. _____
_____

7. _____
_____

8. _____
_____

The participant has demonstrated or identified opportunities to demonstrate learning.

Signed: _____ Participant

_____ Program Facilitator

Learning Support Contract

Part 4

Write down what you will do differently on the job as a result of the program you have just been on:

1. _____
   _____

2. _____
   _____

3. _____
   _____

4. _____
   _____

Part 5

Write down what support you will require to achieve the above:

1. _____
   _____

2. _____
   _____

3. _____
   _____

4. _____
   _____

Signed: _____ Participant

           _____ Participant's Supervisor

Time required

60 to 90 minutes.

Size of group

Unlimited, but large groups need to be broken into teams of 5 to 7 participants.

Material required (for each team)

1 egg (uncooked in its shell).

2 balloons.

1 pair of scissors.

1 ruler.

4 ruled index cards.

4 elastic bands.

10 straws.
6 paper clips.

2 plastic cups (e.g. polystyrene).

10 cm (4 inches) sticky tape.

6 sheets of newspaper.

1 metre (3 feet) length of string.

1 disposable shopping bag (to put everything into).

Overview

An interesting and fun activity that can be used to link into a discussion of issues such as team building, communication, management development and customer service.

Goals

1. To have team members work as a group.

2. To have team members participate in a problem-solving activity.

3. To encourage the group.

4. To have lots of fun!

Procedure

1. Select a suitable test site for this activity—for example, a playing field, hallway or grassed area.

2. Start by breaking the large group into teams of 5 to 7 participants.

3. Tell the teams that they will be participating in a competitive activity and you will give them a kit of materials. Using only the material supplied in the kit, they are to construct an anti-grenade that won't even break the shell of an egg.

4. Tell participants that every anti-grenade must have an egg inside it. Tell them that, after they have constructed their anti-grenade, they will evaluate it. At a test site outside, they must throw their anti-grenade a distance of at least 6 metres (20 feet) without breaking the egg inside it. The anti-grenades must be thrown, not rolled. They must come to a standstill by themselves, not be caught.

5. Give the teams 45 minutes to construct their anti-grenades. Advise them that, if they decide to test their design before you say so, any material destroyed will not be replaced.

6. Your briefing may be something like this:

Your teams are finalists in a list of tenderers for the supply of landing devices to be used on spacecraft in future NASA programs. The tender documentation indicates that you are all equally qualified to produce these items. The final selection will be made today. You have all been asked to come here today to create what the NASA program refers to as an anti-grenade. An anti-grenade is basically a device that doesn't explode on impact. Using only the materials provided, you are to construct a landing device that is safe enough to carry an egg and not break it on impact. Your anti-grenade must contain an egg. If the egg doesn't break when your anti-grenade is tested, you will be awarded a NASA contract. However, if the egg doesn't survive, neither will your chances. The evaluation will require you to throw your anti-grenade at least 6 metres (20 feet) without breaking the egg inside it. Obviously, another factor in our final selection will be the distance the anti-grenade travels. The anti-grenades must be thrown, not rolled. They must come to a standstill by themselves, not be caught. The evaluation will take place in 45 minutes at the test site (tell them where this will be). Good luck!

7. After the teams have constructed their anti-grenades, take them to the test site for the evaluation to take place. Award the winning team the Top Gun title (and perhaps also a Top Gun trophy). Be prepared for lots of laughter.

Sample debriefing questions

Who won?

What went wrong?

What assisted the planning phase?

What hindered the planning phase?

How could you improve the process?

How does this apply to the workplace?

Variations

1. Add or delete items in each team's kit.

2. Have teams estimate, at the end of the planning and construction phase, how far they can throw their anti-grenade without breaking the egg. The team that successfully throws their anti-grenade the estimated distance (or further) wins the Top Gun award.

Facilitator's notes

Time required

30 to 40 minutes.

Size of group

Unlimited, but large groups need to be broken into teams of 5 to 7 participants.

Material required

1 large plain white tee-shirt for each participant.

1 set of coloured (permanent ink) laundry markers for each team.

Overview

You can use this exercise early in the program to help build a team atmosphere.

Goals

1. To enable participants to meet each other in their teams early in the program.

2. To get participants working together.

3. To develop a team atmosphere.

Procedure

1. When the program's initial introductions are complete, break the large group into teams of 5 to 7 participants.

2. Give each participant a plain white tee-shirt.

3. Give each team a set of laundry markers.

4. Tell the teams that they have 20 minutes to create a team name and design a logo for themselves. They are to draw their team name and logo on all of their tee-shirts.

5. When they have finished, ask each team to model the tee-shirts for the group, and explain what their logo is and why they selected it. Encourage teams to wear their tee-shirts for the rest of the day. Facilitators may choose to create a team name and logo for themselves.

Sample debriefing questions

What is the logo?

Why was it selected?

Variations

For groups that may not be very artistic, just get them to select a team name and put that on their tee-shirts.

Facilitator's notes

Time required

30 to 45 minutes.

Size of group

Unlimited.

Material required (for each team)

1 chair.

1 broom or mop (the type where the handle screws into the mop or broom head).

1 set of keys on a ring about 2.5 cm (1 inch) diameter. It's important that, when attached to its head, the broom or mop handle does not quite fit inside the keyring.

The screw end, however, will fit inside the keyring.

1 rope, 16 metres (52 feet) long.

A number of other items, e.g. a flower pot, cup, packet of biscuits, scissors, rubber band, book and newspaper.

Overview

This challenge can be used to demonstrate a problem-solving strategy and to develop lateral thinking.

Goals

1. To look at a problem-solving strategy.

2. To demonstrate how to encourage creative ideas.

Procedure

1. Start by asking for 2 volunteers.

2. Ask both volunteers to leave the area for the time being. They need to be well out of hearing range and where they can't see what you're doing.

3. Set up the props. Place the chair in the centre of an open area. Place the set of keys, with the ring sticking up, on

the chair. Place the length of rope on the ground about 2 metres (6 feet) away from the chair, and form it into a circle around the chair. The rope border around the chair will be about 4.5 metres (15 feet) in diameter.

4. Ask the first volunteer to rejoin the group.

5. Tell them that their task is to get the set of keys from the chair. The only rules are that they are not allowed to cross the rope boundary, they can only use the broom or mop as a tool to assist them, and the keys are not allowed to touch the floor.

6. Give the volunteer the broom or mop and ask them to perform the task. The rest of the group is to observe.

7. After the volunteer fails to succeed with the apparent solution (trying to spear the tip of the broom or mop handle into the ring on the bunch of keys), they will look for other ways to solve the problem. They may end up hooking the broom or mop head around one of the chair legs so that they can drag the chair (and the keys on it) over to the rope border.

8. When the volunteer does solve the problem, congratulate them but tell them that was not the solution you were looking for. Reset the chair and keys, and ask them to try again.

9. Keep them going until they arrive at the solution you are after, which is for them to unscrew the mop or broom handle and use its tapered end to lift the ring of keys.

10. After they achieve this, ask the second volunteer to rejoin the group.

11. Reset the props, and given the second volunteer the same set of instructions except this time tell them that they can use all the items to assist them. Do not specify the broom or mop is the only tool they can use—this time it is only one among many.

12. Keep the second volunteer going until they get the required solution. It may take some time, but eventually they will arrive at it.

13. You can now lead a discussion about issues such as predictability, frustration and lateral thinking.

Sample debriefing questions

Were the first solutions predictable? Why?

How did each volunteer feel during the exercise?

What did the rest of the group observe?

How did the volunteers feel when they arrived at a solution only to be told it was wrong?

Was it unfair to give a lot of irrelevant items to the second volunteer? Does this happen in the workplace?

How does this activity relate to our work environment?

Variations

Have the rest of the group write down as many solutions as they can think of while the volunteers are trying to find a solution, but make sure they do this in silence.

Facilitator's notes

50. The Moat

Time required

5 to 30 minutes (it varies enormously between groups).

Size of group

Unlimited, but large groups need to be broken into teams of 5 to 7 participants.

Material required (for each team)

8 timber or metal stakes.

2 pieces of timber, each 5 cm x 10 cm x 2 metres (2 inches x 4 inches x 6 feet).

1 rope a bit more than 8 metres (27 feet) long.
1 rope a bit more than 25 metres (82 feet) long.

1 hammer.

1 tape measure.

Overview

Here is a challenge in teamwork and lateral thinking.

Goals

1. For participants to experience a teamwork activity.

2. To introduce lateral thinking.

Preparation

1. First you need to select a suitable area of ground in which you can build for each team a square island with a wide moat around it.

2. The island will be exactly 2 metres (6 feet 6 inches) square. Construct the island by putting 4 stakes into the ground to form the square. Make sure these stakes don't stand too far out of the ground.

3. To indicate the edge of the island, tie the 8 metres (27 feet) of rope around all 4 stakes.

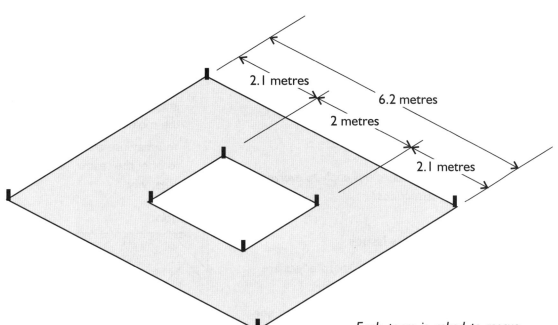

2.1 metres

6.2 metres

2 metres

2.1 metres

Each team is asked to rescue someone who is being held captive inside a castle. The castle sits on a square-shaped island that has a crocodile-infested moat around it. The only way to access the island is across the drawbridge, but it has been raised to stop your rescue operation. You have searched the area and found 2 planks. These planks are the only items available to assist you. Your task is to get to the island safely and rescue the person who is being held captive. The problem is how are you going to cross the crocodile-infested moat? If you touch the water, you can assume you will be eaten (and therefore your rescue will fail)! Good luck!

4. The moat around the island will be exactly 2.1 metres (6 feet 10 inches) wide. To construct the moat around the island, put the other 4 stakes in the ground and tie the 25 metres (82 feet) of rope around all 4 stakes.

5. Place the 2 lengths of timber just outside the outer rope.

Procedure

1. Break a large group into teams of 5 to 7 participants.

2. Give the teams their briefing:

Sample debriefing questions

How long did it take to come up with a solution?

Is this the only solution?

What was the process?

How does this apply to everyday situations?

Safety issues

Make sure all sharp edges are taken off the timbers.

Watch to make sure no one trips on the stakes in the ground.

Variations

1. This activity may be used either outdoors or indoors.

To set it up indoors, just put some masking tape on the floor in place of the ropes and stakes. Use your imagination when creating the moat!

2. You may use a different story to brief the teams, but use creativity.

Solution

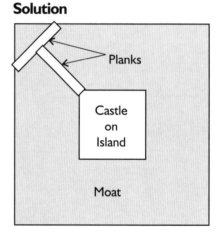

Planks

Castle on Island

Moat

Facilitator's notes

Time required

10 to 20 minutes.

Size of group

Unlimited, but it's best to break large groups into teams of 5 to 7 participants.

Material required (for each team)

1 pipe, about 30 cm (12 inches) long, with an inside diameter slightly bigger than a ping-pong ball.

1 ping-pong ball.	1 unopened can of soft drink.
1 large shifting spanner.	1 plastic shower screen.
1 carpenter's saw.	1 tennis ball.
1 ball of string.	2 rolls of toilet paper.
1 small jar of honey.	1 unopened bottle of wine.
2 sheets of writing paper.	2 ceramic cups.
2 pens.	4 unused party balloons.
1 pair of reading glasses.	2 raw eggs
	1 small chilli plant

It's probably not practical to have all of these items with you. In that case, give each team a copy of the list and get them to use their imagination!

Overview

An interesting and thought provoking activity designed to get participants working together.

Goals

1. To get participants to work together.

2. To develop lateral thinking.

3. To demonstrate the benefits of synergy (working together).

Preparation

For each team, put a pipe into the ground so that it stands upright about 25 cm (10 inches) above the surface. If you are going to use this activity more than once on your own property, you could have the pipes set in concrete. Each time you've finished with them, cover them over so no one trips over them.

Procedure

1. Show the teams the pipes that you embedded in the ground.

2. Place a ping-pong ball in each pipe.

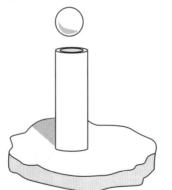

3. Tell the teams their task is work out how many ways they can think of to retrieve the ping-pong ball without damaging it, the pipe or the ground. Tell them they have

searched the area and found the items listed above. They may use any or all of these items to assist them with their task.

4. After they complete this activity, you can lead a discussion about strategies and solutions.

Sample debriefing questions

How may solutions did you find? Would they all work?

How did you generate ideas?

Did each team develop ideas in addition to individuals' solutions? Why?

How does this activity relate to everyday activities?

Safety issues

Remove the pipes after the activity to ensure that no one trips over them.

Variations

1. Use your imagination to think of a variety of other items you could use instead of those listed.

2. You can start this activity by having each participant find

their own solution, and then have them work on team solutions.

Solutions

There are many possible solutions, including the following.

1. Pour the soft drink and/or the wine into the pipe to make the ping-pong ball float to the top.

2. Put some honey on the end of the string and use that to lift the ping-pong ball out of the pipe.

3. Get some chillies off the chilli plant, dry out the seeds, put them in the pipe and water them so the growing plant lifts the ping-pong ball out of the pipe.

Facilitator's notes

Time required

20 to 30 minutes.

Size of group

Unlimited, but large groups need to be broken into teams of 8 to 12 participants.

Material required

None, but participants may like to find suitable items if they wish.

Overview

Here is an activity that encourages groups to bond from the outset.

Goals

1. To identify each small group.
2. To encourage communication.
3. To allow individuals in each group to bond with one another.
4. To have fun!

Procedure

1. Have the large group break into teams of 8 to 12 participants.
2. Ask each team to come up with a name for itself within 10 minutes. The name may be practical or symbolic.
3. Ask each team to introduce themselves to the group, telling everyone their team name and why they chose it.
4. Use the team names for the duration of the course.

Sample debriefing questions

What were the names?

Did the names chosen accurately describe each team?

Will this exercise improve the course? Why?

Variations

Group members could be rotated during the program.

Facilitator's notes

Time required

1 hour plus.

Size of group

Unlimited, but large groups need to be broken into smaller teams of 5 to 7 participants.

Material required (for each team)

1 length of 12 mm (¹/₂ inch) diameter rope, about 10 metres (30 feet) long.

1 broom handle, about 2.4 metres (8 feet) long (or a tree branch of similar size)

1 pole, about 2.4 metres (8 feet) long x 5 cm (2 inches) diameter (or a tree trunk of similar size).

1 hardwood plank, about 4 metres (12 feet) long x 20 cm (8 inches) x 5 cm (2 inches).

1 bucket, half full of water.

An area with a bank, about 1.2 metres (4 feet) high (for the teams to work from). Use a porch or veranda if you can't find a bank to work from.

Overview

Here is a seemingly impossible task for a team to perform—although they will find it relatively easy once they get under way.

Goals

1. To demonstrate the power of synergy (working together).

2. To develop team spirit.

3. To have the team complete a seemingly impossible task.

Procedure

1. Start by breaking the group into teams of 5 to 7 participants. Ask for a volunteer from each team to be an observer.

2. Have each team stand on the bank and place the bucket so that it's not too easy for them to reach—that is, it's achievable with a bit of imagination and a bit of stretching.

3. Explain their task to the teams. They have to retrieve the bucket using only the materials provided. They are not allowed to leave the bank where they are standing. In other words, they can' t simply send someone down to get it. If anyone touches the ground below the bank during the exercise they will immediately be blinded. This exercise will only be successful if the bucket is retrieved without spilling any of the water in it.

4. You could use this brief for this challenge:

Your team is on an expedition into a remote part of Treasureland. There is an ancient city located deep in the jungle. After many months of searching, you have finally found the city. The problem is that the city itself has started to sink and the lower parts of the land are covered with a rare microscopic spore. If this spore touches a human, it causes immediate blindness. While looking into the depression, your team has noticed an ancient vase. This vase is the Vase of Venus. It is rumoured that the Vase of Venus contains an incredible assortment of valuable jewels and coins. Your team has decided to try to take the vase with them. The problem is to retrieve it without touching the ground or the spores. You have been able to find these items to assist you (point out the items). These are the only items you can use. If you spill the contents of the vase, it is rumoured that a curse will descend on you. Avoid this at all costs. The wind looks as though it's increasing in speed, so it's important that you complete your task as soon as possible—the strong winds could blow the spores into the air, and that would be disastrous. Time is running out, so good luck with the retrieval.

Sample debriefing questions

What was the problem? How did you break it down? Who did what?

What helped solve the problem?

What problems did you encounter?

Who took on what roles?

Did the team work effectively?

How could it have functioned better?

Safety issues

This activity requires constant observation.

Variations

Include some useless materials to add confusion, e.g. a small branch with some leaves on it or an empty soft drink can (ancient of course!).

Solution

One possible solution looks something like this:

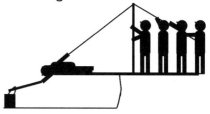

Facilitator's notes

Time required

I hour plus.

Size of group

8 to
20 participants.

Material required

2 lengths of 20 mm
($^3/_4$ inch) diameter
rope, both about
30 metres
(100 feet) long.
The less stretch
the rope has, the
better.

I large area with
well-established
trees that are
reasonably close to
one other.

Overview

This activity is designed to
challenge the individual, while
developing team support.

Goals

1. To challenge the individuals in
    a group.
2. To develop team support.

Preparation

1. You will need to set up this
    activity before the program
    commences. Select an area
    that contains several trees
    which are strong enough to
    take the load of several
    participants without bending.

2. Take one length of rope and

tie it off firmly on a tree trunk about 1 metre (3 feet) above ground level. Take the rope to another tree, about 3 to 4 metres (10 to 12 feet) away. Pull the rope tight and make a couple of turns around the trunk, then do the same to several more trees until you run out of rope. Tie the rope off firmly on the last tree. Get the second length of rope and go back to the first tree. Using the same procedure, tie the second rope between the trees about 3 metres (10 feet) above ground level.

3. Make sure you tie off the beginning and end of each rope firmly. What you should end up with is 2 lengths of rope that link the trees: one rope will be one metre off the ground and the other will be about 2 metres above the first rope.

Procedure

1. Take the group to the area you've already set up.

2. Explain the group's task. Participants have to move from one end of the rope to the other end without touching the ground. If anyone touches the ground, the whole group must start again.

3. Your briefing might go something like this:

Your team has been out on a long bush walk. On your way back you came across this toxic wasteland. One of your group has identified the substance on the ground to be extremely poisonous. The consequence of touching it could be fatal. It is getting dark so there isn't enough time to go back another way. You must go forward. Someone has obviously been here before you as there are ropes tied off between the trees. These trees span the toxic area. The group has to cross the wasteland without touching the ground. Should anyone touch the ground, you must all come back and start over.

Sample debriefing questions

Did everyone survive?

Who thought they wouldn't be able to achieve this task? Why?

Did team members support each other?

What was helpful?

Safety issues

It's a good idea to have a couple of spotters for this activity. You can explain that they're able to walk over the toxic area, as they're wearing special toxin-resistant shoes—and, no, they can't be used by anyone else!

You may want to tie off the first rope a little lower—say half a metre (18 inches) from the ground—for some groups, but keep the second rope about 2 metres above it.

Variations

You can blindfold several participants. This will obviously lead to other questions in the debriefing.

Facilitator's notes

Time required

10 to 20 minutes.

Size of group

Unlimited.

Material required

1 large grassed area.

Overview

This is a group activity to get everyone involved in attempting a world record push-up.

Goal

To have the group work on a cooperative activity.

Procedure

1. Ask for 4 volunteers. Check to make sure that each volunteer is capable of doing at least one push-up and does not have any back problems. You can use as observers anyone who doesn't want to participate, who can't do a push-up or who can' t participate.

2. Have the 4 volunteers do a group push-up. To do this, ask them to lie on the ground and then assume the push-up

position but with their feet on each other's backs. If they do this correctly, when they do their push-up, there should be no feet on the ground—just their 4 pairs of hands.

3. Once the 4 volunteers have accomplished this first push-up, ask the rest of the group to get involved. Add one participant at a time to the group push-up. Start each new attempt with everyone lying on the ground. Their aim is to get as many people as they can to do a giant push-up.

Sample debriefing questions

What was the problem? How did you break it down? Who did what?

How does this activity relate to the workplace?

Safety issues

Don't allow anyone with a back problem to participate in this activity.

Variations

After the group's final attempt, ask them to extend their world record by moving, in formation, a distance of 3 metres (10 feet).

Facilitator's notes

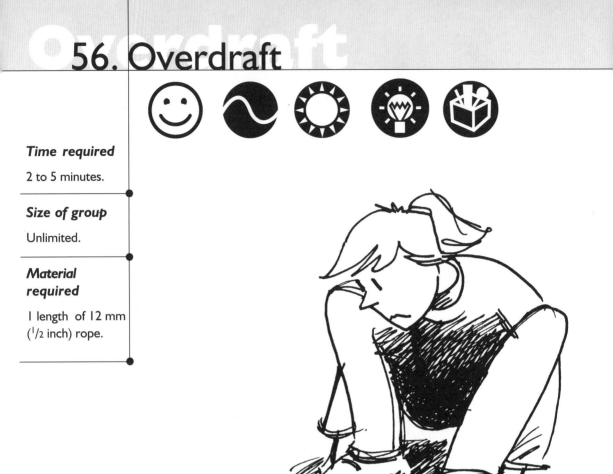

Time required

2 to 5 minutes.

Size of group

Unlimited.

Material required

1 length of 12 mm (¹/₂ inch) rope.

Overview

Here is a fun activity that you can use at the start of the program.

Goal

To show people that even the very best of us fail at some activities.

Procedure

1. Lay the rope in a straight line along the ground.

2. Ask everyone in the group to stand 30 cm (12 inches) away from the rope.

3. Ask them to bend over and grab on firmly to the ends of their feet with both hands.

4. Their task is to jump over the rope without letting go of their feet. Tell participants that, if anyone can do this, they will win a brand new $10 note. They must jump forwards, not roll or fall, and they must keep hold of their feet.

5. After everyone has given up, tell them that there may be times when they can't 'win' during activities in the program. Point out that winning or losing isn't the most important thing—it's more a matter of learning through the process. Some tasks may *seem* impossible— and they may be impossible, but they may not be. Tell participants to focus on the process and have fun at the same time!

Sample debriefing questions

Is it possible to perform this task?

What is the purpose of this exercise?

How does this activity relate to what we are about to get involved in?

Facilitator's notes

Time required

15 to 20 minutes depending on the size of the group and the course selected.

Size of group

Unlimited.

Material required

2 balloons, plus spares, for each team.

1 large obstacle course (it could go around trees, or over and under tables, or over fences and large grassed areas—whatever you choose, make it challenging!)

1 whistle.

Overview

If you have any balloons left over during your program, here's a way to use some of them.

Goals

1. To have teams participate in a competitive exercise.
2. To energise the group.

Procedure

1. Have everyone in the group select a partner.
2. Give each pair 2 balloons and ask them to fully inflate one of them. Ask one partner to put the other balloon in their pocket.
3. Now tell each pair their task

is to take the inflated balloon through an obstacle course. Tell them where the course goes. Advise them that the first pair to complete the course with their balloon still intact will be declared the winners. The rules are that they must keep their balloon in the air at all times—they are not allowed to hold on to it. If the balloon touches the ground, they have to return to the beginning and start again. If they break their balloon, they must stop where they are, get their spare balloon out and inflate it fully before they can continue. If they move while they are still inflating their balloon, they must go back to the beginning and start again.

4. Blow your whistle to get them started.

5. Here is a brief you may consider using:

You and your partner landed on the moon. While you were both outside on a moon walk, you found an unusual object and decided to take it back to the landing module. Unfortunately you're unable to carry this object. However, because of the moon's lack of gravity, you can hit it into the air and not have it fall immediately to the ground. Your mission is to get the object back to the landing module without it touching the ground. If it does, you must go back to the beginning and start again. If you burst the object, you must create a new one before being able to continue. Good luck and have a safe mission!

Sample debriefing questions

Who finished first?

What strategies did you use?

Did anyone cheat?

Does anyone feel as though they lost? Why?

Did each pair work as a team?

Safety issues

Participants will be looking up at the balloon for most of this activity, so ensure that there isn' t anything on the ground for them to trip over.

Variations

Ask each pair to keep 3 balloons aloft during the activity. You can do this as a second round.

Facilitator's notes

58. Poles Apart

Time required

15 to 30 minutes.

Size of group

Unlimited.

Material required (for each participant)

1 blindfold.

Overview

Here is a great activity to build trust between partners.

Goals

1. To build a sense of trust between partners.

2. To develop team spirit.

Procedure

1. Ask everyone in the group to select a partner.

2. Give one partner in each pair a blindfold.

3. Take everyone to one end of a field. Point out an object near the other end of the field.

4. Tell the pairs their task is for one partner to walk to the object without looking while their partner walks behind them to make sure they don't fall or bump into anything. Ask the partners with the blindfolds to put them on. Tell the sighted partners that they are not to give their blindfolded

partners any directions or suggest where they should walk. Once the blindfolded partner gets to the point where they think the object is, they are to stop and see how close (or far away) they are from it.

5. Ask the pairs to repeat the activity, this time swapping roles. Once they have all had a turn at both roles, ask them why most participants were so far off target.

6. Suggest to them that it may work better if they do it in pairs. Hand out a second blindfold to each pair. Everyone should now have a blindfold. Ask each pair to look at the object, put their blindfolds on, link arms or hold hands, and try again. Make sure you have a camera for this, you'll get some great shots to take back to work!

7. After they see that it doesn't work much better doing the activity in pairs, suggest that the whole group try it together. Have them all look at where the object is, hold onto each other and try to get there as a group. Tell the group that when they get to

where they think the object is, they should stop and leave their blindfolds on.

8. When the group has stopped, ask everyone to point in the direction where they think the object is. Ask them to keep pointing in that direction while taking off their blindfold with their free hand.

9. Now tell the group why this activity is called Poles Apart—it's because a compass can point in many directions when it is located at one of the poles. Also mention that, although the individuals may have had different ideas on where the target was, the group as a whole would have got closer to it than most of the earlier individual or pair attempts.

Sample debriefing questions

Why did the group get closer to the target than the individuals or pairs?

What does this suggest?

Safety issues

Ensure there are no obstacles for people to trip over.

Variations

Have participants walk backwards towards their target.

Facilitator's notes

59. Funny Face

Funny Face

Time required

5 minutes.

Size of group

Unlimited.

Material required

A handful of small coins.

Overview

You can use this game at any time during a program to introduce a bit of humour, or to relieve tension after a serious activity or discussion.

Goal

To get participants laughing.

Procedure

1. Have the group stand in a circle with everyone facing inwards, including yourself.

2. Ask for about a half of the group to volunteer to start this exercise. Have them move into the centre of the circle and lie down. Each volunteer should lie flat on their back with the back of their head touching the ground.

3. Go inside the circle with the volunteers. Tell them they must keep their head and body completely still. They

are not allowed to lift their head off the ground or move it from side to side.

4. Place a small coin on the tip of each volunteer's nose.

5. Their task is to use only facial contortions to get the coin off their nose within one minute. Make sure you have a camera handy, you'll get some great facial shots to put on the noticeboard back at work!

6. After the one minute, ask the group to swap roles and repeat the activity.

7. If some participants are successful, have them lie on the ground in a circle with their heads all pointing towards the centre of the circle (preferably with their heads touching one another), and see who is the fastest to dislodge the coin.

Variations

To make it more challenging, and more fun, use 3 coins and place one on each volunteer's nose, forehead and chin.

Facilitator's notes

60. Comets

Time required

10 to 20 minutes.

Size of group

Unlimited.

Material required

1 stocking or pair of pantyhose for each team.

1 tennis ball for each team.

1 large playing field.

Overview

Ever wondered how you can recycle pantyhose and stockings? Probably not, but here's something you can use them for.

Goal

To have small teams participate in a competitive exercise.

Procedure

1. Start by taking the group to one end of an open field. Ask everyone to form pairs.

2. Give each pair a stocking (or pantyhose) and a tennis ball.

3. Ask each pair to slide the tennis ball into the toe of the stocking and tie off the stocking immediately behind the ball. Ask them to make this into a 'comet' by stretching the stocking so that it forms a tail away from the tennis ball.

4. Their task is for one partner to throw the comet and for the other to catch it. They are allowed to hold only the comet's tail—not the tennis ball—both to throw and to catch. The aim is to see which pair can throw the comet furthest.

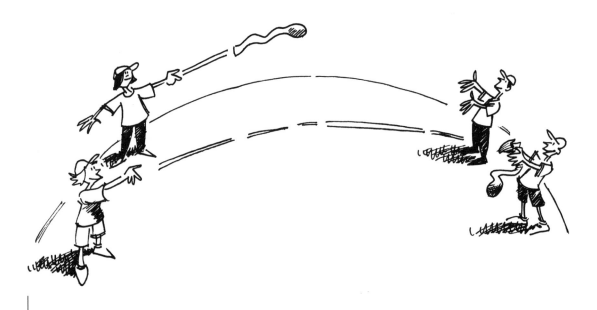

5. Give the pairs 10 minutes to prepare themselves.

6. Have each team perform in front of everyone else to see who throws furthest.

Sample debriefing questions

Which team threw furthest?

What was the problem? How did you break it down? Who did what?

Did each pair work as a team?

Safety issues

These balls will get up quite a bit of speed, so keep each throwing pair well clear of the rest of the group. If the area isn't big enough to do this, use the trick that golfers use. Tell everyone that, if their comet looks as though it's going to hit someone, they should sing out 'Fore'. If anyone else hears this, they are to take up the 'anti-comet position' and to put up their 'comet shields'—that is, crouch down and put their hands over their heads!

Variations

You may prefer to use teams of 3 instead or pairs for this activity. In this case, each team will have one thrower and 2 catchers.

Facilitator's notes

Time required

5 to 10 minutes.

Size of group

Unlimited.

Material required

None.

Overview

Here is a quick, competitive exercise that doesn't require any props.

Goal

To have participants compete with each other.

Procedure

1. Have everyone select a partner.

2. Ask each pair to stand facing one another. Each participant should have their feet together and stand about an arm's length away from their partner.

3. Ask each partner to put their arms out and join palms with their partner. They are not allowed to touch their partner anywhere else during the activity.

4. Each pair's task is to try to get their partner off-balance. A participant is considered off-balance if they move their feet. Each time this happens, their partner scores one point. If both partners are off-balance, neither scores. A participant loses one point if they touch their partner anywhere other than their palms.

5. Tell the pairs to get ready and then sing out: 'Go'.

Sample debriefing questions

Who was the best in each pair? Why?

What strategies worked best?

What does this activity tell us about competition?

How does this activity relate to the workplace?

Variations

1. Tell the teams that no fast moves are allowed.

2. Pair the 'winners' from each partnership, and have them compete with each other in another elimination round. Repeat until you have a champion of champions.

Facilitator's notes

62. ESP

Time required

5 minutes.

Size of group

Unlimited.

Material required

None. However, if you have a group that likes to 'cheat', you may consider using blindfolds.

Overview

This is the ultimate cooperative exercise. You simply can't do it without a partner.

Goal

To demonstrate the power of ESP (extrasensory perception).

Procedure

1. Ask everyone to select a partner.

2. Have each pair face one another, standing about 1 metre (3 feet) apart. Ask each participant to put one hand out and touch their partner's hand, then put their hand back down by their side.

3. Tell participants they are to do the rest of this exercise in complete silence.

4. Ask everybody to close their eyes tightly and spin around 3 times, then face where they think their partner is standing and put their hand up to touch their partner's hand.

Sample debriefing questions

Who was able to touch their partner's hand?

How did you do it?

Do some people really have ESP?

Safety issues

Some people have a problem with spinning around. If that's the case, use them as spotters.

Variations

Conduct this exercise a second time, with participants doing it in teams of 3.

Facilitator's notes

63. Masters Classic

Time required

20 to 40 minutes.

Size of group

Unlimited, but large groups need to be broken into teams of 3 participants.

Material required

1 frisbee for each team.

1 large playing field.

Overview

If you like playing golf, you'll love this game. If you don't like playing golf, you'll still love it because you're not playing golf.

Goal

To have teams work in a cooperative exercise.

Procedure

1. Take the group to one end of the field. Have participants form teams of 3 participants.

2. Give each team a frisbee and tell them that they will be playing frisbee golf.

3. Point out a tree, or other object, at the other end of the playing field. Tell participants it is their target.

4. Tell them the rules. They must start at this end of the field. One person in each team throws the frisbee, and either of the other 2 team-mates must catch it before it hits the ground. If the frisbee hits the ground without

being caught, one of the catchers must take it back to the thrower for them to throw it again from exactly the same position. If the frisbee is caught before it hits the ground, the person catching it must remain where they are. They become the thrower, and throw the frisbee to their team-mates who are now the catchers. Each team's task is to hit the target at the other end of the field with the lowest possible score.

5.   Here's how the scoring works. Each team gets one point for a throw with a successful catch. Add a point each time their frisbee hits the ground.

6.   Allow the team 2 minutes planning time, and then start the game.

Sample debriefing questions

Which team had the lowest score?

Did you have enough planning time at the start?

What strategies did you use?

Did the team work effectively?

Safety issues

Advise participants to keep an eye out for flying frisbees.

Variations

1.   Participants can play this game in pairs rather than teams of 3. Alternatively, it can be played in larger teams. Regardless of how big the team is, there is only one thrower—everyone else is a catcher.

2.   Place another target on the starting line, and ask teams to play a second round on the way back.

Facilitator's notes

64. Water Balloon Ball

Time required

5 to 10 minutes.

Size of group

Unlimited.

Material required

1 balloon for each pair.

Water (to fill the balloons).

1 large playing field.

Overview

This activity is ideal for a lively group on a hot day—it's designed for having fun.

Goals

1. To develop team spirit.
2. To have participants compete with each other..

Preparation

Partly fill each balloon with about 1 litre (1 quart) of water. Let any air out, and tie off each balloon.

Procedure

1. Start by having everyone select a partner.

2. Have each partner stand about 2 metres (6 feet) apart, facing one another, so that the pairs form 2 lines.

3. Give one partner in each pair a water-filled balloon.

4. Ask them to toss the balloon to their partner so they catch the balloon without it bursting.

5. After they have done this successfully (most will), have one line take a giant step backwards. Ask them again to throw the balloon to their partner without it bursting. Keep repeating this until only one balloon remains intact. The winning pair can do whatever they like with their balloon.

Sample debriefing question

Which pair threw their balloon furthest?

Safety issues

Not a good activity for a cold and windy day!

Variations

When balloons bursts and one partner is soaked, suggest they share the experience with their partner by hugging them.

Facilitator's notes

65. Contagious

Overview

Here is a fast moving game for having fun.

Goals

1. To energise the group.
2. To have participants interact physically without being self-conscious.

Preparation

You need to mark out the boundaries of the playing area beforehand.

Procedure

1. Tell the group that this activity is similar to the game Tag. Explain that this game starts with one participant as the catcher and everyone else trying to avoid being caught. The catcher is to 'tag' another player by touching them. When they've done this, both players join hands, and the tagged player becomes the catcher. The new catcher tags another player, they join hands and so on. Play continues until the last player has been caught.

2. Here is a brief you might use:

One of your team members is going to be infected with a rare contagious disease. This disease causes your hands to produce a powerful glue. If you have the disease and touch someone else,

you are forced to join hands with them. This link cannot be broken. If they touch someone else, they are forced to join hands with them as well. This disease also affects a person's logic. Instead of trying to isolate the disease, they have an obsession with passing it on to others. Your challenge is to remain free as long as possible. Good luck!

3. Point out the boundaries of the playing area, take the tennis ball out of your pocket and throw it to one participant. Tell them that the ball contains the virus and they have now been infected (you have been immunised and therefore are unaffected by it).

Sample debriefing questions

Who survived the longest?

How did the group feel about this activity?

Safety issues

Watch to make sure participants at the end of the line of linked players don't lose their balance.

Variations

You can tell the group that after the virus has infected 4 participants, it splits them into 2 sets of 2 players each. Each set continues to grow until they number 4, when they split again, and so on.

Facilitator's notes

Time required

45 minutes.

Size of group

Unlimited.

Material required

1 cord or similar for each pair (to tie 2 ankles together).

2 cords or similar (to tie 2 pairs at the waist)

1 playing area (football field or similar).

1 soccer ball (or similar).

1 whistle.

Overview

If participants like playing outdoor sports and don't mind a bit of running around, they will enjoy this activity.

Goals

1. To have participants work cooperatively in pairs and in teams.
2. To energise the group.
3. To have participants interact physically without being self-conscious.

Procedure

1. Start by breaking the group into 2 teams of equal numbers. If there is an odd number of participants, have one volunteer to be your assistant.

2. Ask all participants to select a partner, preferably of similar size, from their own team.

3. Ask each participant to tie, at the ankles, one of their legs to one of their partner's legs.

4. Have one pair from each team stand back to back, and tie them together around the waist. They will be the goalkeepers for each team.

5. Explain the rules. Participants will play a game of soccer in 2 halves of 15 minutes each. At half time, the teams will swap ends. All players are to remain tied at the ankles for the duration of the game. They can use any of their '3' legs to kick the ball. Soccer rules will apply (if you don't know them, ask the group or make them up).

6. Answer any questions and blow your whistle to start the game.

Sample debriefing questions

Which team won?

What problems did you encounter?

How did the partners work together?

What made the teams work together more effectively?

Safety issues

Use anyone who does not want to play as a linesperson.

Before the game starts, encourage participants to practise moving around while they are tied together.

Variations

1. You can play the second half with participants tied in groups of 3 rather than in pairs.

2. You can have one partner in each pair wear a blindfold.

Facilitator's notes

Time required

15 to 20 minutes.

Size of group

Unlimited.

Material required

1 length of rope.

1 whistle.

Overview

Here is a round robin activity that can be used at any time during your program.

Goals

1. To have participants compete with each other in a fun way.

2. To have participants interact physically without being self-conscious.

Procedure

1. Start by laying the rope along the ground in a straight line.

2. People with back problems should not participate in this exercise. Have the group form a single line with the tallest person at one end and the shortest at the other end, then start at one end and work along the line pairing partners of equal size. Obviously if there is an odd number of participants, you will have to join the line.

3. Have each partner stand on either side of the rope.

4. Ask everyone to turn around so that they are facing away from their partner.

5. Ask the partners to bend over, put their arms between their legs and hold each other's hands. The rope should remain between each partner.

6. Their task, once they hear you blow the whistle, is to try to pull their partner over the rope—just like in the game tug of war.

7. Have the winners then form partnerships, and repeat the activity until you have an overall winner and lots of smiling faces.

8. Ask everyone to go back to their first partner and take up their original position. Their task is to push their partner back far enough so that they can step over the line themselves. Repeat this until you have an overall winner.

9. As a finale, have a group tug of war. Ask everyone to resume their original position, but this time have each partner bend over and cross their arms so that they hold hands with 2 participants (their partner with one hand and another player with the other hand) that are behind them. The first team to pull the other team over the line is the winner.

Sample debriefing questions

What was the problem? How did you break it down? Who did what?

How does this activity relate to the workplace?

Safety issues

People with back problems should not participate in this exercise.

Ensure participants are gentle with one another.

Facilitator's notes

Time required

10 minutes.

Size of group

Unlimited.

Material required

1 frisbee for every participant.

1 large grassed playing area.

Overview

Here is a simple activity that can be used at any time—it's like musical chairs, but uses frisbees.

Goals

1. To have some fun.
2. To energise the group.

Procedure

1. Start by laying each frisbee on the ground several metres apart.

2. Explain that participants are to walk around the playing area chanting or singing while keeping a good distance from the 'islands' (that's the

frisbees). When you sing out 'South Pacific', players are to get to an island as quickly as they can. The last person to get to an island is out of the game. Players are not allowed to touch one another when they are trying to get to an island. Anyone who does this is also out of the game.

3. Repeat the activity, reducing the number of islands as the group gets smaller, until only one player remains. Declare this player the overall winner.

Variations

If you have a CD or cassette player, play music and have participants make for the islands when you stop the music.

Facilitator's notes

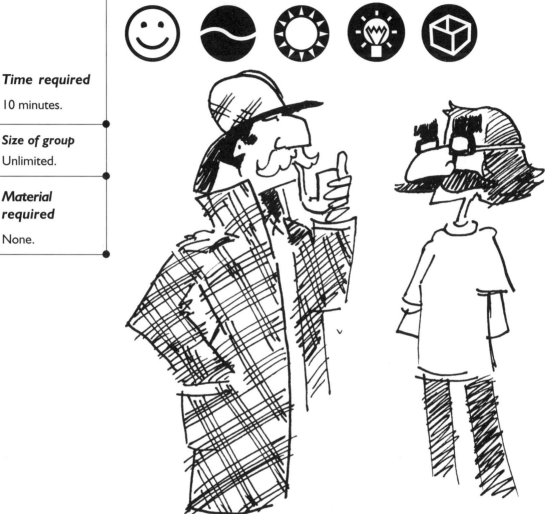

Time required

10 minutes.

Size of group

Unlimited.

Material required

None.

Overview

Here is a good exercise to use at the opening of a program. It demonstrates how unobservant people can be, and how they need to improve their powers of observation during the program.

Goal

To demonstrate how observant participants are.

Procedure

1. Have all participants form pairs.

2. Ask each participant to look at their partner for one minute.

3. After one minute, ask participants to turn away so that they cannot see their partner.

4. Ask everyone to alter up to 7 items of their appearance—these can be subtle or dramatic changes.

5. Ask participants to face their partners once more. They are now to take turns, attempting to identify all of the changes their partner made.

Sample debriefing questions

How many participants picked all of their partner's changes correctly?

Why is it that most didn't pick all the changes immediately?

How does this relate to the activities we have coming up?

How does this activity relate to the workplace?

Facilitator's notes

70. Tidal Wave

Time required

15 to 20 minutes depending on the number of participants.

Size of group

Unlimited, but a minimum of about 20 participants.

Material required

None.

Overview

Here is a trust exercise that doesn't require any props.

Goals

1. To build trust within a team.

2. To work as a team by helping each other.

3. To have participants interact physically without being self-conscious.

185

Procedure

1. Ask the group to form 2 lines. Participants in each line should stand shoulder to shoulder and as close as they can to the person in front of them (the person in the other line). If there is an odd number of participants, have one be your assistant.

2. Select one participant at the front of the line as the 'traveller'. Ask the group to lift this participant up and pass them overhead, hand by hand, along the 2 lines of 'lifters'. This really is a case of 'many hands make light work'. When the traveller gets to the end of the line, the last few lifters should ensure that the 'traveller' has a safe landing by supporting their torso while they place their feet on the ground.

Sample debriefing questions

What did you feel about the activity initially?

How do you feel now that you have attempted it?

How did you feel while you were being passed along?

Safety issues

Have as many spotters as necessary. This will depend totally on the type of group you have.

Variations

If you have a small group, ask the people at the front of the line to move to the back as soon as they have passed the 'traveller' back. This way you can move the 'traveller' from one spot to another.

Facilitator's notes

Time required

30 minutes plus.

Size of group

Unlimited.

Material required

1 quoit (or similar).

1 headband or armband for each participant (equal numbers of headbands or armbands in each of 2 colours).

1 stopwatch.

1 large playing field.

Overview

The main ingredient in this activity is energetic participants.

Goals

1. To energise the group.
2. To have the group compete in teams.

Procedure

1. Ask the group to form 2 teams of equal size. If there is an odd number of participants, have one be your assistant.

2. Give each team one set of the headbands or armbands.

3. Show the teams the boundaries of the playing area.

4. Tell participants their team's aim is to maintain possession of the quoit for 30 seconds. Tell them the rules. You will throw the quoit into the air to start play. The first player to catch the quoit takes possession of it. If they are 'tagged' (touched) by a member of the opposing team, they must stop moving immediately and pass the quoit to another member of their own team within one second. If they take any longer to pass on the quoit, the referee (that's you) will take the quoit and restart play. If members of opposing teams catch the quoit at the same time, the referee will

also restart play. When one team gets close to maintaining possession for 30 seconds, the referee will count out loud '5, 4, 3, 2, 1' to let the other team know that they need to move quickly to take possession. If other rules are required (and they will be) make them up as you go!

Sample debriefing questions

How did each team perform?

What roles did participants take? Who were the doers, thinkers and carers?

Safety issues

Make sure the quoit (or similar) is not too hard, so it doesn't do too much damage if it hits someone. Alternatively, use a tennis ball or other small, low-impact ball.

Variations

1. Vary the 30-second possession requirement according to the size of the playing area.

2. If headbands or armbands are not available, use some other means of distinguishing the 2 teams, e.g. the colour of their shirts, their hair colour, or whether their sleeves are up or down.

Facilitator's notes

Time required

1 hour plus.

Size of group

Unlimited, but large groups need to be broken into teams of 6 to 8 participants.

Material required (for each team)

3 hardwood planks 25 cm (10 inches) x 5 cm (2 inches) x 2.7 metres (9 feet) long.

1 length of 1 cm (¹/₂ inch) diameter rope about 6 metres (20 feet) long.

7 bricks or blocks set out as shown on the next page

Overview

Here is a classic problem-solving activity that everyone enjoys.

Goals

1. To have the team participate in a problem-solving activity.

2. To encourage the team to work together.

3. To demonstrate the benefits of synergy (working together).

Preparation

Prepare for this activity before the program commences. If you're going to use this activity more than once on your own property, set it up permanently using timber poles fixed into the ground instead of the bricks or blocks. Feel free to make the set-up bigger, as this makes it more interesting. Looking at the set-up, there should only be one way for

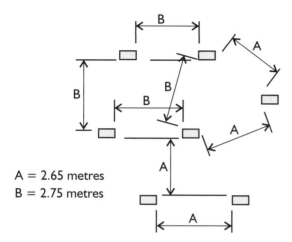

A = 2.65 metres
B = 2.75 metres

participants to lay the planks so that they fit between the bricks.

The planks should fit in the spaces marked 'A' in the diagram. The planks should not fit in the other spaces (marked 'B' in the diagram) because these spaces are just a little bit shorter than the planks. Because of this small difference in size, participants will not be able see which way to go at a glance. In fact they shouldn't be able to see any difference in them—this makes the problem more difficult.

Procedure

1. Start by selecting a team of 6 to 8 people. Take them to the starting area and give them their brief.

2. Your brief may be something like this:

Your team has just crash landed on a distant planet. On impact, your spaceship broke in two. You are currently standing with one part of the spaceship. The other part of the spaceship, containing the radio, spare air, food and first aid equipment is on the other side of what looks like a cosmic slop. As we all know, cosmic slop is deadly. It's essential that you all get to the radio to call for help. No one is to be left behind. After scouting the area, all your team has been able to find are 3 pieces of timber (from a solar tree) and a length of rope from your part of the spaceship. That's all the equipment you have to perform the task. As you know, if anyone touches the cosmic slop, the consequences are horrific. The timber from the solar tree and the rope are also affected by the cosmic slop. If they touch it, they will dissolve immediately. You will see that there are several solar rocks, they look like bricks, laying on the ground. These cannot be moved, however you may place planks on them if necessary. They will offer protection from the cosmic slop. If the bricks are moved, they will release a corrosive gas that will affect your spacesuits. You only have 30 minutes to get across before your air runs out. Good luck!

3.   If anyone touches the ground with their body, the planks or the rope during the activity, have the entire team start again.

Sample debriefing questions

What was the problem? How did you break it down? Who did what?

How did you solve the problem?

What roles did people take on?

Was there any conflict? If there was, how you did resolve or deal with it?

What problems did you encounter? How did you overcome them?

Did the team work effectively together?

What does this activity tell us about teamwork?

Safety issues

Make sure the edges of the planks have been sanded back so they have no sharp edges.

As there will probably be 6 to

8 people standing on one plank, make sure that the planks are strong enough to support their weight without breaking.

If you use hardwood planks, as suggested, you will find them to be reasonably heavy. As a result, make sure participants use correct lifting and handling techniques.

Variations

You can make the activity more difficult if you need to challenge the group. Identify the team's natural leader beforehand, tell them that they have been temporarily blinded during the crash landing, and ask them to wear a blindfold.

Solution

This is one possible solution:

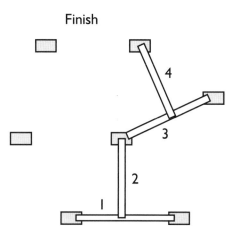

Finish

Start

The numbers 1 to 4 indicate the order in which participants need to place the planks on the bricks. They can place plank 1 on the two bricks by hand. They would probably tie a rope to one end of plank 2, then stand it up on plank 1 and lower it onto the next brick. They would do the same with plank 3. With plank 3 in place, everyone would have to move out onto it. Then they would need to retrieve plank 2 so they can use it as plank 4. With the last plank in place, everyone can finish the walk across. It's that simple!

Facilitator's notes

Time required

30 to 40 minutes.

Size of group

16 to 30 people.

Material required

1 tall tree with branches (to tie a swing rope on).

1 length of rope (the swing rope) that is strong enough to take the weight of the heaviest participant.

1 length of timber or string (to mark the starting point).

1 prepared platform.

Have the platform constructed out of solid timber (a piece of 20 mm ($^3/_4$ inch) plywood, about 60 cm (24 inches) square, with pieces of timber screwed to the bottom). The pieces of timber on the bottom are to lift the plywood off the ground and give it additional strength. This platform will hold 12 to 16 participants. If you have a larger group, make the board a bit bigger (but not too big).

Overview

If you've ever tried to see how many people you can fit into a telephone box, you'll know how much fun this activity can be—and it's a bit more challenging.

Goals

1. To involve participants in a team problem-solving activity.
2. To have participants interact physically without being self-conscious.

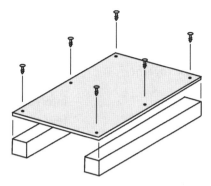

Preparation

1. You need to set up a swing rope that enables participants to swing from the tree to the platform. Select a suitable tree branch (make sure it is strong enough) and tie the rope securely to it. The rope should be long enough to swing from the starting line to the platform.

2. Work out the swing area (the safest arc for participants to swing across). At one end of the swing area, place the length of timber or string on the ground. If string is used, it's best to put stakes at each end of the string and tie it off so that it's taut. This line indicates the starting point.

3. Place the platform about 4 metres (12 feet) away from the starting line. It should be positioned so that people can swing from the starting line over to it.

Procedure

1. Have the group stand around and tell them what they have to do. They will have 10 minutes to prepare for this activity. What they need to do at the end of that time is to establish a new world record for the number of people that can fit on to a platform of this size without any of them touching the ground or any person still on the ground touching or supporting them in any way. Let them know that, for safety reasons, participants may not be stacked on top of each other. The only way to get to the platform is to swing out to it. If anyone touches the ground on the way out, they must come back and try again.

2. After the 10 minutes planning, ask the group to tell you what their target is, and then have them try to achieve it.

Sample debriefing questions

What was the problem? How was it broken down? Who did what?

What roles did people take?

Did everyone participate?

How did the team work together?

Safety issues

Make sure there are no sharp edges on the timber platform and no screw heads sticking out.

Do not allow participants to be stacked on top of one another—otherwise those at the bottom will finish up with a huge weight on top of them and may find it very difficult to breathe!

Variations

1. This is yet another activity that can be made more interesting by blindfolding a few of the team members. It's even more interesting if you blindfold their natural leaders!

2. Position the platform so that participants can't swing in a direct line from the starting point.

Facilitator's notes

Time required

30 to 60 minutes.

Size of group

Up to about
24 people.

Material required

A tree with a
branch that's
suitable to hold a
swing rope.

A length of rope
(strong enough to
take the weight of
the heaviest
participant).

1 length of timber
or string (to
represent the cave
entrance).

1 plywood disc,
about 30 cm
(12 inches) in
diameter, for every
participant.

Life on a String

Overview

This activity will get participants working together and their blood moving. Its focus is teamwork and communication.

Goals

1. To improve teamwork.
2. To involve the team in a problem-solving exercise.
3. To have participants interact physically without being self-conscious.

Preparation

1. Before this activity commences, prepare the area. Start by tying the rope to the tree branch (make sure it's strong enough). The rope should be long enough to reach the area immediately outside the 'cave entrance' when you put it in place.

2. Once you have positioned the swing rope, work out the preferred direction for participants to swing in. At one end of the swing area, mark the 'cave entrance' by placing the length of timber or string on the ground. If you use string, it's best to put a stake at each end and tie the string off so that it's taut.

3. Place all the plywood discs on the ground, spreading them out evenly in the swing area.

Procedure

1. Give the team their briefing. Your briefing could be something like this:

You all remember watching Raiders of the Lost Ark. Inside the cave there were pressure sensitive sections on the floor. If they were touched, nasty things started to happen. Here we have something similar. To gain access to the lost treasure, we need to have one person stand on each of the discs that are on the ground. We just can't walk out to them because, similar to Raiders of the Lost Ark, the floor area around the discs is pressure sensitive. If you touch the floor area, those nasty things will start happening again. The rope on the ground indicates the cave opening. The only way to get to the discs is to swing out to them using the rope. As soon as one person lands on a disc, they must keep pressure on it. This means that once you land on a disc, you cannot move from it until every disc has someone on it. When you achieve that, the cave wall will open to reveal the hidden treasures. Your first problem is to get the rope, which is hanging from the ceiling of the cave. Remember, no one is allowed to touch the floor. Good luck!

2.   If anyone touches the ground around the discs, the team has to start over again.

3.   Once the exercise is complete, you can lead a discussion about teamwork and problem-solving.

Sample debriefing questions

What was the problem? How did you break it down? Who did what?

What helped to achieve the result?

What problems did you encounter? How did you overcome them?

Did any leaders emerge?

What does this exercise demonstrate?

How does this activity relate to the workplace?

Safety issues

Usually knots are not allowed to be tied in the swing rope. If your participants are reluctant or young, it may be worthwhile putting one knot near the end of the rope about 1 metre (3 feet) above ground level so that they can put the rope between their legs to help support them.

Variations

1.   If there are more than 24 participants, use the others as observers, or set up additional swing areas.

2.   You can set a time limit for this activity. Tell participants that, once someone lands on the first disc, there's only 15 minutes until the cave will close, never to be opened again.

3.   Conduct this activity indoors, using a climbing rope in a gymnasium.

Facilitator's notes

Time required

30 to 60 minutes depending on the size and skill of the group.

Size of group

Unlimited, but large groups need to be broken into teams of 10 to 12 participants.

Material required

1 pole, 15 cm (6 inch) diameter x 5 metres (15 feet) long.

2 substantial trees, about 20 cm (8 inches) in diameter and 3.5 to 4 metres (10 to 12 feet) apart.

Overview

Here is a team initiative that requires everyone to be involved as a participant, observer or spotter.

Goals

1. To involve everyone in a team challenge.

2. To build trust within the team.

3. To have participants interact physically without being self-conscious.

Preparation

Before the program commences, bolt the pole securely to the 2 trees so that it's about 2.4 metres (8 feet) off the ground. Make certain the pole is secure because it needs to bear the weight of up to 3 participants at a time during the challenge.

Procedure

1.. Give the teams their briefing. Here is a brief you may use:

Clint Eastwood made a great escape from Alcatraz. Your escape doesn't have to be as complex. Just imagine that your team has been locked up for many years. One day out in the exercise yard, you notice that there are no guards around. All that remains between you and freedom is a wall that's 2.4 metres (8 feet) high. You all agree to try to get as many as possible of your team over the wall. You've estimated that you have about 15 minutes before your escape attempt will be noticed. Good luck!

2. Tell the teams that, for everyone's safety, no one is allowed to be thrown over the pole, no one is allowed to dive over the pole, and only 3 people are allowed on the pole at any one time.

3. Ask everyone who is not involved in the escape attempt to be a spotter.

Sample debriefing questions

How successful were the teams at completing the challenge?

What was the problem? How did you break it down?

What roles did people take?

Did the team work together effectively? Why?

What problems did you encounter? How did you overcome them?

What helped the teams to perform their task?

Safety issues

People will try anything to 'escape'. Keep a close watch (and listen closely) to ensure no one is thrown over the pole, no one dives over the pole and no more than 3 people at a time are on the pole.

Variations

If you need to challenge the group further, blindfold one or two participants in each team to make it much more difficult. Tell these participants that they have just come from the prison hospital, where they were administered strong eye drops. If you blindfold participants, ensure you have plenty of capable spotters in place when they try to go over the pole. Remind the spotters that their role is to closely watch other participants in the activity, so the spotters can give them some protection if they fall. The spotter's first priority is to protect the participant's upper body by offering physical support.

Facilitator's notes

TRAINING INFORMATION

We offer a comprehensive range of training services around the world. If you would like more information on our training services, please complete the information below and forward it to us by mail, fax or email.

Name: _____

Position: _____

Company: _____

Address: _____

_____

_____

Phone: _____

Fax: _____

Email: _____

I would like more information on:

☐ In-house Presentation Techniques Skills Seminar

☐ Public seminar information for Presentation Techniques Skills Workshops

☐ In-house Training Techniques Workshops

☐ Public seminar information for Training Techniques Workshops

☐ In-house Time Management Seminars

☐ Public seminar information for Time Management Seminars

☐ Public seminar information on other subjects

☐ In-house Training Games Workshops

Post to:	Gary Kroehnert
	Training Excellence
	PO Box 3169
	Grose Vale, NSW 2753
	Australia
Or fax to:	(02) 4576 0700
Or email:	doctorgary@hotmail.com

Introducing other training titles by Gary Kroehnert

The Training Games Series

How can I enhance a team's performance?

How do I improve an individual's perception?

How do I energise? break the ice? improve communication?

Australia's best-selling training author and consultant, Gary Kroehnert, presents a four volume collection of games and activities designed to promote structured workplace learning through simulations, role plays and exercises for individuals and teams.

These games are suitable for trainers, facilitators, supervisors, human resource managers and consultants who wish to expand their collection of proven ideas and learning exercises.

Basic Training for Trainers 3/E
A Handbook for New Trainers

What do I need to know to be a good trainer? How can I achieve my training objectives with maximum results? How do I know if my training methods are working? Could my sessions be improved?

This third edition training bestseller is a must-have for trainers at all levels. Using his trademark clear and entertaining writing style, Gary Kroehnert explains everything you need to know about training—from the core principles of adult learning to communication, preparation and research.

ORDER FORM   McGraw-Hill

Phone: (02) 9415 9888   Fax: (02) 9417 7003

http://www.mcgraw-hill.com.au/mhptr

OR MAIL THIS ORDER FORM

	0.07.470434.6	Greenwich	The Fun Factor	37.95
	0.07.470770.1	Greenwich	Fun & Gains	32.95
	0.07.470606.3	**Kroehnert**	**Basic Presentation Skills**	**32.95**
	0.07.470662.4	**Kroehnert**	**Taming Time**	**32.95**
	0.07.452770.3	**Kroehnert**	**100 Training Games**	**37.95**
	0.07.470749.3	**Kroehnert**	**101 More Training Games**	**37.95**
	0.07.470802.3	**Kroehnert**	**102 Extra Training Games**	**37.95**
	0.07.4710508	**Kroehnert**	**103 Additional Training Games**	**37.95**
	0.07.470913.5	**Kroehnert**	**Basic Training for Trainers 3/e**	**37.95**
	0.07.470768.X	Leigh & Kinder	Learning Through Fun & Games	37.95
	0.07.471051.6	Leigh & Kinder	Fun & Games for Workplace Learning	37.95
	0.07.470842.2	Zeus & Skiffington	The Complete Guide to Coaching at Work	32.95
	0.07.471103.2	Zeus & Skiffington	The Coaching at Work Toolkit	32.95

NAME

TITLE

COMPANY

ADDRESS

POSTCODE

Payment Details

I enclose payment by (please tick):

☐ Cheque   ☐ Credit Card   ☐ Company Purchase Order

☐ Bankcard   ☐ American Express   ☐ Mastercard   ☐ Visa   ☐ Diner's Club

Card Number ☐☐☐☐☐☐☐☐☐☐☐☐☐☐☐☐   Expiry Date ☐☐☐

Signature

Phone, fax or mail your order to

McGraw-Hill Australia Pty Ltd

4 Barcoo Street Roseville NSW 2069 Ph: (02) 9415 9888 Fax: (02) 9417 7003

Email: cservice_sydney@mcgraw-hill.com.

Please ensure you have enclosed payment with your order. If you fax your order please do not post it as well.